MAX notes

KU-245-368

Victor Hugo's

Les Misérables

Text by
Suzanne Uber
(B.A., Bloomfield College)
Department of English
Bridgewater-Raritan High School
Bridgewater, New Jersey

Illustrations by
Thomas E. Cantillon

Research & Education Association

MAXnotes™ for
LES MISÉRABLES

Printed in the United States of America

Library of Congress Catalog Card Number 94-65959

International Standard Book Number 0-87891-951-1

MAXnotes™ is a trademark of
Research & Education Association, Piscataway, New Jersey 08854

What **MAXnotes**™ *Will Do for You*

This book is intended to help you absorb the essential contents and features of Victor Hugo's *Les Misérables* and to help you gain a thorough understanding of the work. The book has been designed to do this more quickly and effectively than any other study guide.

For best results, this **MAXnotes** book should be used as a companion to the actual work, not instead of it. The interaction between the two will greatly benefit you.

To help you in your studies, this book presents the most up-to-date interpretations of every section of the actual work, followed by questions and fully explained answers that will enable you to analyze the material critically. The questions also will help you to test your understanding of the work and will prepare you for discussions and exams.

Meaningful illustrations are included to further enhance your understanding and enjoyment of the literary work. The illustrations are designed to place you into the mood and spirit of the work's settings.

The **MAXnotes** also include summaries, character lists, explanations of plot, and chapter-by-chapter analyses. A biography of the author and discussion of the work's historical context will help you put this literary piece into the proper perspective of what is taking place.

The use of this study guide will save you the hours of preparation time that would ordinarily be required to arrive at a complete grasp of this work of literature. You will be well-prepared for classroom discussions, homework, and exams. The guidelines that are included for writing papers and reports on various topics will prepare you for any added work which may be assigned.

The **MAXnotes** will take your grades "to the max."

Dr. Max Fogiel
Program Director

Contents

> **Each section includes List of Characters, Summary, Analysis, Study Questions and Answers, and Suggested Essay Topics.**

SECTION ONE

Introduction

The Life and Work of Victor Hugo

Victor Hugo (1802-1885) was the most influential and best known of the nineteenth century French poets. A poet, novelist, and dramatist, he was a leader of the Romantic movement in France. Born in 1802, Victor was a sickly child who was the youngest of three sons. His father was a soldier of the Revolution whose military career required the family to move often after Napoleon's rise to power. After his parents separated when he was 16, Victor lived with his mother, a royalist and conservative, whose political views strongly influenced him. He reconciled with his father after her death in 1821.

Recognized as a child prodigy, Hugo became a prolific and successful writer at an early age. His first published volume of poems led to an annuity of 1200 francs from King Louis XVIII, a sum permitting him to marry Adele Fancher, his childhood sweetheart. They were to have two sons and two daughters.

Hugo's early dramas also expanded his reputation. In 1829, his drama *Marion de Lorme* was censored because of its negative portrayal of Louis XIII. When the romantic drama *Hernani* was staged soon after, his fellow writers and other artists organized to support it. Throughout his career, Hugo challenged not only established literary conventions, but also the governments under which he lived. The publication of *The Hunchback of Notre Dame* in 1831, a long novel about medieval Paris, enhanced his prestige and popularity.

In 1833, Hugo fell in love with Juliette Drouet and she became his mistress. Their affair lasted 50 years and inspired some of his lyric poetry. *Claude Guex,* published in 1834, expressed Hugo's interest in the social problems caused by poverty as well as his views on abolishing the death penalty. In 1841, he was honored by being elected to the French Academy.

Hugo began work on *Les Misérables* in 1845, but his work was interrupted by the Revolution of 1848. Initially, he supported the conservative party and Napoleon's son, Louis Napoleon, for the presidency, but he broke with both over social and political issues. In 1851, when Louis Napoleon declared himself Emperor Napoleon III, Hugo began a 19-year exile which led him first to Jersey and later to Guernsey where he collaborated with other artists and writers also in exile. Many of them were offered pardons and returned to France, but Hugo rejected amnesty and continued to criticize the government from abroad.

During this period, he wrote some of his greatest works, including nature poetry and poems inspired by his daughter Leopoldine, whose drowning in the Seine following a boating accident in 1843 was a great tragedy. His most famous novel, *Les Misérables*, was published in 1862 and received instant acclaim.

Hugo remained in exile until the downfall of Napoleon III in 1870 when he returned to Paris with Juliette. He continued to publish novels, poetry, and plays until he was in his eighties. When Juliette died of cancer in 1883, his health began to deteriorate, and he died two years later in May of 1885. His body lay in state beneath the Arc de Triomphe, an honor usually reserved for heads of state, and all of France mourned the man who had been the favorite author as well as the conscience of the nation. He left an extraordinary number of completed works which were published after his death.

Historical Background

The end of the eighteenth century was marked by massive social and political change as rebels took up arms in both America and France. The Industrial Revolution of the mid 1700s, based on scientific advances of the Enlightenment, ushered in the Age of Reason. People thought science would improve life for everyone.

The storming of the Bastille, a prison for political prisoners, on July 14, 1789, marked the beginning of the French Revolution. France became a constitutional monarchy based on the ideals of "liberty, equality, and fraternity" set forth in the Declaration of the Rights of Man. Two years later, the monarchy was overthrown and King Louis XVI sent to the guillotine. What followed was a Reign of Terror. Chaos prevailed and thousands died as royalists and rebels competed for power.

Napoleon Bonaparte came to power in 1799, seizing control of the army and declaring himself emperor. Although he was defeated at the Battle of Trafalgar when he led his army against the British in 1807, his campaigns in Europe gave him control of almost all of Europe. Napoleon was finally defeated in 1815 at the Battle of Waterloo. Royalists rejoiced as monarchies were restored throughout Europe while radicals mourned the defeat of the principles of the revolution.

Literature reflected the dramatic events of the time, moving from an emphasis on science and the practical to an emphasis on the idealistic and the emotional. Writers of the Romantic Age focused on the concerns of the individual and the common man rather than on the needs of society as a whole. Reacting to the social evils of the ongoing Industrial Revolution, they placed a new emphasis on nature. Whereas writers of the past had seen evil as an innate part of man, Romantic writers believed in the inherent goodness of man.

Influenced by other Romantic writers, Victor Hugo wrote *Les Misérables* against the backdrop of the French Revolution and the events which followed. Many of the characters in the novel had real life models, including Pontmercy, who was patterned after Hugo's father, and Marius and Cosette, who reflected Hugo himself and his wife. The bishop in the novel was modeled after Monsignore Miolles of Digne who also helped a criminal to escape.

In his preface, Hugo sets forth "three problems of the age—the degradation of man by poverty, the ruin of woman by starvation, and the dwarfing of childhood by physical and spiritual night" which he attempts to address in the novel. Each of these conditions is represented by one of the characters, and Hugo uses them to comment on the social conditions of his day. Though its primary theme is society's treatment of the unfortunate, the novel is also about redemption.

Master List of Characters

Jean Valjean—*The protagonist. The plot centers around his life after he is released from serving a 19-year prison term. Also called Father Madeleine, Monsieur Madeleine, Monsieur the Mayor, Urbain Fabre, Monsieur Leblanc, and Ultimus Fauchelevent.*

Jacquin Labarreh—*The host of the inn La Croix de Colbas who refuses to serve Jean.*

Madame la Marquise de R—— —*The woman who meets Jean in Cathedral square. She gives him four sous and advises him to knock at the bishop's door.*

The Bishop of D——, Monseigneur Bienvenu—*A truly Christian man, he offers Jean refuge and shows faith in him. A symbol of good, he influences the struggle raging in Jean's heart between good and evil.*

Madame Magloire—*The bishop's servant.*

Mademoiselle Baptistine— *The bishop's sister who fears Jean but follows her brother's lead and makes him welcome.*

Maubert Isabeau—*The baker in Faverolles who catches Jean stealing a loaf of bread from his shop.*

Petit Gervais—*A 12-year-old street musician. Jean meets him on the plain and steals a silver 40-sous piece from him. Regretting his action, Jean searches in vain for him for years.*

The Thénardiers—*Paris innkeepers paid by Fantine to raise Cosette. After they lose their inn, they move to Gorbeau House and assume the name Jondrette.*

Eponine—*The oldest daughter of Thénardier. She is in love with Marius but helps him to find Cosette. At the barricade she is mortally wounded when she deliberately stops a bullet intended for Marius.*

Azelma—*Thénardier's younger daughter who eventually goes to America with him.*

Fantine—*Cosette's mother who is unable to care for her child because she must find work in a factory.*

Laffitte—*The banker of M——sur M——.*

Javert—*The antagonist. A policeman in M——sur M—— who pursues Jean Valjean.*

Father Fauchelevent—*Jean jeopardizes himself by rescuing this old man when his horse and cart tip over on him. Fauchelevant later repays him by providing shelter in the convent.*

Father Champmathieu—*This peasant is arrested for stealing apples and incorrectly identified as Jean Valjean.*

Brevet, Chenildieu, Cochepaille—*The three convicts who testify against Champmathieu and swear he is Jean Valjean.*

M. Baloup—*Master wheelwright who employs Champmathieu but cannot be located to testify on his behalf.*

Sister Simplice and **Sister Perpétue**—*The nuns who care for the dying Fantine. Sister Simplice lies to Javert to protect Jean.*

The old portress—*Servant of Jean Valjean when he was the mayor.*

The old landlady—*The landlady of Gorbeau House. She is called Ma'am Bougon by Courfeyrac.*

Cosette—*The daughter of Fantine. Jean rescues her from the evil Thénardiers and raises her as if she were his own child. She falls in love with and marries Marius.*

M. Gillenormand—*The grandfather of Marius who raises him. He is an elderly bourgeois gentleman who is a royalist.*

Mademoiselle Gillenormand the elder—*The oldest daughter of Gillenormand. Never married, she lives with her father and nephew Marius and keeps house for them.*

Lieutenant Théodule Gillenormand—*Mademoiselle's nephew who spies on Marius for her.*

George Pontmercy—*A brave and decorated soldier of the revolution who is one of Bonaparte's colonels. Married to Gillenormand's younger daughter, he agrees to give up their son Marius after her death so the child will not be disinherited.*

Marius—*Pontmercy's son who is raised by his grandfather and aunt. Not until after his father's death does he learn to love his father and understand his politics.*

Abbé Mabeuf—*The priest who is curé of Vernon. He befriends Colonel Pontmercy and tells Marius about his father.*

Courfeyrac—*A friend of Marius, he teaches him English and German and introduces him to the publisher who gives him a job. He is one of the revolutionists.*

Touissant—*Rescued from a hospital by Jean, this old woman becomes the servant of Jean and Cosette.*

Gavroche—*Thénardier's son, one of the band of insurgents. His small stature allows him to move in and out of the barricade without being noticed.*

Enjolras—*One of the commanders of the insurgents.*

Bossuet, Feuilly, Combeferre, Joly, and **Bahorel**—*Some of the revolutionists at the barricade.*

The portress—*A servant in Jean's building.*

The physician— *He attends to Jean.*

Summary of the Novel

Set in the post-Napoleonic era just after the French Revolution, *Les Misérables* is the story of Jean Valjean, a convict, who has just been released from prison after serving 19 years for stealing a loaf of bread. Influenced by the bishop to begin a new life, Jean assumes a new name and moves to a new location where he becomes a respected citizen and makes a fortune in manufacturing. The police inspector, Javert, is suspicious of him, but it is not until Jean's conscience prods him to reveal his true identity that he is forced to flee.

The rest of the novel is set in Paris, where Jean changes residences frequently and assumes a number of identities in order to avoid arrest. Fulfilling a promise to her dying mother Fantine, he rescues a young girl named Cosette from the evil Thénardier family and becomes her guardian. They spend many years in a convent where Cosette grows into a beautiful young lady. Eventually, Jean leaves this safe haven so that Cosette may have a more normal life.

Cosette falls in love with Marius, a young lawyer, who joins a band of revolutionists at a barricade. Unbeknownst to Marius, Jean is also at the barricade; when he is wounded, Jean, who has spared the life of his constant adversary Javert, risks his life to carry Javert to safety through the sewer system of Paris, returning him to his family and Cosette.

Against all odds, Jean struggles to follow the bishop's teachings and become a good man. It is not until after the wedding of Cosette and Marius and he is on his deathbed that he is at last able to stop running from his past and reveal all. Not until then does he finally find peace.

Estimated Reading Time

Because of its length, the complexity of the plot, and its many unfamiliar terms, the average student will require at least eight hours to read *Les Misérables*. The novel is comprised of five main parts, four bearing the name of a main character and one named for the setting of that part. Each part is divided into a number sections named to advise the reader of the direction of the plot. These sections are further subdivided into shorter subsections. Readers should pay particular attention to the titles of each subsection which provide clues regarding the action.

First-time readers of the novel are advised to tackle no more than one part at each sitting. The first three sections introduce the main characters as well as the plots and subplots. The final two sections are considerably longer and more complicated as the author ties everything together and progresses toward the final resolution. Readers are well advised to break each of these sections into at least two sittings.

This MAXnotes study guide is based on the 1961 abridged edition by James K. Robinson.

SECTION TWO

Fantine

The Fall

New Characters:

Jean Valjean: *the main character*

Jacquin Labarre: *host of the inn*

Madame la Marquise de R——: *the woman in the square*

Madame Magliore: *the bishop's servant*

Mademoiselle Magliore: *the bishop's sister*

Maubert Isabeau: *the baker of Faverolles*

Petit Gervais: *a street musician from Savoy*

Summary

One evening a weary traveler enters the small town of D——
in a western region of France near the French Alps. His clothes are
ragged and torn, and he is exhausted from walking all day. The time
is October 1815. He stops briefly at the mayor's office and then
searches for shelter for the night.

He visits an inn called Le Croix de Colbos where the host,
Jacques Labarre, offers him dinner and lodging. Labarre writes a
note on a scrap of paper and sends a child out of the inn with it.
When the child returns with a reply, the innkeeper abruptly refuses
service. The stranger protests until the innkeeper identifies him as
Jean Valjean and indicates that he knows who he is.

Valjean next seeks shelter in a tavern, in the local prison, and in the home of a young couple. Turned away by all, he finally crawls into a hut only to discover that it is a dog house. Despondent, he wanders out of town and into a field. The barrenness of the countryside, the contours of a twisted tree, and gloomy light images reflect the hopelessness of his situation.

Returning to town, he finds a stone bench in Cathedral square and lies down. An old woman, Madame la Marquise de R——, comes out of the church. She gives him four sous and advises him to knock on the door of the bishop.

The Bishop of D——, his servant, Madame Magliore, and his sister, Mademoiselle Baptistine, are preparing for the evening meal. The women discuss the necessity of calling the locksmith to put bolts on the door. Madame Magliore has heard talk in town of the arrival of a vagabond and they are afraid. Before the discussion ends, there is a knock on the door and the bishop says, "Come in!"

Jean Valjean enters and immediately confesses that he is a convict who was released from prison four days ago after serving 19 years — five for burglary and 14 for four failed escape attempts. He has walked 12 leagues (a league is equal to three miles) from Toulon and is going to Pontarlier. He tells them that his yellow passport, which he is obligated to present to the mayor's office, identifies him as a convict and prevents him from finding shelter.

Valjean is astonished when the bishop not only offers him dinner and a place to sleep but also shows him respect by calling him *monsieur*. The bishop tells him, "This is not my house; it is the house of Christ." Madame Magliore places two silver candlesticks on the table and serves supper, which Valjean eats ravenously.

After dinner, the bishop takes one of the silver candlesticks from the table. He hands the other to his guest and leads him to an alcove behind his own chamber where Jean Valjean falls into a deep sleep.

Awaking in the middle of the night, Valjean reflects on his past. Born in Brie, France, both of his parents died when he was young. His father, also named Jean Valjean, was a pruner who died after falling from a tree, and his mother, Jeanne Mathieu, died from milkfever. Raised by his older sister, Jean was just 25 when she became a widow. Thereafter, he supported her and her seven children.

Unable to read, Jean too became a pruner in the town of Faverolles. He earned 18 sous a day during the pruning season. The rest of the year he worked in a variety of other jobs. During the harsh winter of 1795 he could find no work and the family had no food. In desperation, he smashed the window of the local bakery and stole a loaf of bread. The baker, Maubert Isabeau, pursued and caught him.

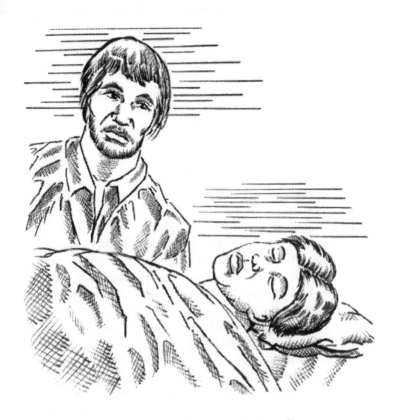

He was tried and sentenced to five years in the galleys.

On April 22, 1796, the same day Napoleon Bonaparte's victory at Montenotte was announced in Paris, Jean Valjean became part of a chain gang. While the iron collar was being riveted around his neck, he wept and raised his hand seven times as if he were touching the heads of his nieces and nephews.

After a 27-day journey, he arrived at the galleys in Toulon, where he was given the clothes of a convict. His past, including his name, was erased, and he was known thereafter as Number 24601.

The fourth year he escaped, but he was captured the following day and given an additional three years. He escaped again the sixth year, and because he resisted when he was caught, five years were added to his sentence. Escape attempts in the tenth and sixteenth years each added three more years. Having served 19 years, he was finally released in October of 1815.

Jean's ecstasy over his freedom was soon squashed when he realized that his yellow passport made him a marked man. The day after his release, he worked at a flower distillery unloading bags. While he was working, he was obliged to show a gendarme (policeman) his yellow passport. Later, the foreman, who paid the other workers 30 sous per day, gave Jean only 15 because his yellow passport.

"Liberation is not deliverance. A convict may leave the galleys behind, but not his condemnation."

Unaccustomed to the softness of a bed, Jean awakens at 2 a.m. He thinks of the six silver plates and the ladle that were on the dinner table and struggles with his conscience. At three o'clock, he rises, picks up his knapsack, and opens the window to observe the garden below. From his sack he removes a miner's drill, a solid iron instrument with a pointed end that he used to quarry stone when he was a convict. Holding the drill, he moves silently to the bishop's unlatched door.

Cautiously, he pushes the bishop's door. A rusty hinge creaks but awakens no one. He reaches the bishop's bed just as a ray of moonlight illuminates the bishop's peaceful expression. Jean, still wrestling with his conscience, is terrified by his radiance. Though he hovers momentarily "between two realms, that of the doomed and that of the saved," he steals the bishop's silver and escapes over the garden wall.

The following morning three gendarmes return Jean and the silver to the bishop who informs them that the silver belongs to Jean. The bishop tells Jean to take the silver with him and counsels him to be good.

Leaving the city, Jean encounters a young musician from Savoy who entertains with a hurdy-gurdy and a marmot. Though Petit Gervais protests and even cries, Jean takes a 40-sous piece from him. Later, Jean tries to find the boy. Overwhelmed by guilt and thoughts of the bishop, he weeps. No one knows where Jean goes that night, but at 3 a.m. the stage-driver observes a man kneeling and praying in front of the bishop's door.

To Entrust is Sometimes to Abandon

New Characters:

Thénardier and Madame Thénardier: *innkeepers*

Eponine: *oldest daughter of Thénardier*

Azelma: *Thénardier's younger daughter*

Fantine: *a young mother seeking employment*

Cosette: *Fantine's child*

Summary

An inn in Montfermeil, near Paris, run by Thénardier and his wife, has a picture over the door depicting a general in the midst of battle. Written beneath are the words "TO THE SERGEANT OF WATERLOO." Part of a carriage, possibly a gun carriage, sits in front of the inn. The wife is watching her daughters play when another mother approaches with her child.

The children play together while the two women chat. The second mother, named Fantine as we will discover in the next chapter, explains that she cannot take her daughter Cosette with her to search for work. She asks Madame Thénardier to care for Cosette for six francs a month. After some negotiations, the Thénardiers agree to keep her for seven francs a month plus an additional fifteen for expenses. The innkeeper uses the money to repay his loan.

The author comments on the character of the Thénardiers who belong to a "bastard class" with none of the attributes of the middle class and all of the vices of the lower class. He reveals that Thénardier, once a soldier, had painted the sign on his inn although he did not do a good job.

Fantine finds employment in M——sur M—— and writes every month for news of her child. After six months, Thénardier demands 12 francs a month and soon raises it to 15. Fantine pays. She does not know that her child's clothes have been pawned and that she is dressed in rags and treated like a servant by the time she is five. Cosette is called The Lark because she is like a small, frightened bird. Sadly, this bird never sings.

The Descent

New Characters:

Laffitte: *the banker*

The old portress: *servant of Jean Valjean*

Javert: *the policeman*

Summary

The year is 1818. Cosette travels to M—— sur M——, her native village, where she finds work in a factory which manufactures imitation English jet beads and German black glass trinkets. Though the factory had been in operation for many years, the business was revolutionized three years before her arrival by a stranger who arrived in the town with almost no money in much the same way as she did. He invented a new manufacturing process which made the factory extremely profitable and made him a rich man. On the day of his arrival, the stranger had risked his own life to save two children from a burning building. Overwhelmed with gratitude, the police neglected to ask for his passport. The man was known thereafter as Father Madeleine.

By 1820, Father Madeleine had 630,000 francs in the Laffitte banking house, and he had donated more than a million to the city and its poor. As his wealth increased, he began to be called Monsieur Madeleine. He was adored by his employees and respected by all. The king pronounced him mayor in 1819 and he was offered the Cross of the Legion of Honor. He declined both honors. The following year he again refused the appointment of mayor but finally yielded when the public insisted. He then became known as Monsieur the Mayor.

Despite his position, he continues to lead a solitary life, secretly doing good deeds and using his free time to cultivate his mind. Several of the young ladies in the town, curious because no one has ever seen his room, ask to see it. They find an ordinary room with two antique silver candlesticks on the mantle.

When newspapers report the death of the 82-year-old Bishop of D——, the mayor wears black. This leads to speculation that he is related to the bishop. When asked, he replies simply that he was

"a servant in his family" when he was young.

Every time a young person from Savoy passes through the town, the mayor sends for him and questions him, hoping to find Petit Gervais. The young Savoyards tell each other that the mayor gives them money, so many of them arrive.

The mayor is highly respected by everyone. People come from miles around to seek his advice and have disputes settled. The local police inspector, Javert, a man feared by the homeless, is suspicious of the mayor, but the mayor treats him kindly.

An old man named Father Fauchelevent is one of the few

people who do not like the mayor. His business is bankrupt, and he is jealous of the mayor's fortune. Left with only a horse and cart, he makes his living by carrying goods for others. One day the horse falters and the cart overturns, pinning him beneath. Bystanders are unable to free him, so Javert sends for a jack.

When Madeleine arrives and learns that it will take a quarter of an hour for the blacksmith to arrive with the jack, he offers money to anyone who will crawl under the cart and lift it. Javert remarks that he has only known one man with that much strength, a convict in the galleys at Toulon. When the cart sinks further into the mud and Fauchelevent begins to scream, the mayor crawls under the cart and uses his great strength to raise it. "Twenty arms" help to lift it and Fauchelevent is saved.

Madeleine carries Fauchelevent to the infirmary in his factory where two sisters care for his broken knee. He leaves a thousand francs and a note saying that he has purchased the horse and cart, not mentioning that the horse is dead and the cart destroyed. He arranges for Fauchelevent to become the gardener in a convent in a district of Paris called Saint Antoine.

The success of Madeleine's business has brought the people prosperity and happiness. The collection of taxes, a measure of public wealth, has become an inexpensive and easy matter. This is the state of the country when Fantine arrives and begins to work in the factory.

Javert

New Characters:

Father Fauchelevent: *an old man*

Father Champmathieu: *a peasant*

Brevet, Chenildieu, Cochepaille: *three convicts*

Summary

Javert confesses to Monsieur Madeleine that he has mistaken him for Jean Valjean and publicly denounced him. He apologizes and tells the mayor that he should be dismissed from his position. Javert says he realized his mistake when a man named Father Champmathieu was arrested for stealing cider apples. In prison, a convict, Brevet, identifies Champmathieu as Jean Valjean. Brevet claims that Champmathieu, like Jean Valjean, is a pruner and that his name combines Jean, pronounced *Chan* in that region, and Mathieu, the family name of Jean's mother. Two other convicts, Cochepaille and Chenildieu, also swear that Champmathieu is Jean Valjean.

Though surprised by this information, Monsieur the Mayor minimizes its importance and refuses to dismiss Javert. Javert agrees to continue in his job.

The Champmathieu Affair

New Character:

M. Baloup: *Champmathieu's employer*

Summary

From the time he arrived in M——sur M——, Jean Valjean had "but two thoughts: to conceal his name and to sanctify his life; to escape from men and to return to God." When there was a conflict between these two goals, he never hesitated to favor the second. This was the reason he risked discovery by doing things like rescuing old Fauchelevent. His conscience dictates that he must go to Arras to save the accused. He must "re-enter into hell" to become an "angel" or become a "devil" by remaining silent.

The mayor goes to the Royal Court at Arras, where he sends a note to the judge requesting permission to witness the trial. The mayor's reputation has spread throughout France, so the judge is honored to admit him.

Entering the court, Jean sees the judges on one side and the lawyers on the other. His attention immediately fixes on the accused. "He thought he saw himself." All the horrors of the past are revived in his memory. The scene is a kind of nightmare vision of the worst moment in his life. He notices that, unlike his own trial, a crucifix hangs above the judge's head. "When he was tried, God was not there."

Valjean sinks into a chair and positions himself behind a pile of papers. The trial has been in progress for three hours. The accused, thought to be Jean Valjean, is charged with a second offense, the robbery of Petit Gervais. He emphatically denies the charge.

In his own defense, the prisoner testifies that he worked as a wheelwright in Paris for M. Baloup. Both he and his daughter worked outdoors, exposed to all kinds of weather for very little money. His daughter, whose husband beat her, worked all day, washing clothes in the river. Sometimes she did laundry indoors where it was warmer, but there her eyes were ruined by hot lye. She is now dead, and M. Baloup is bankrupt and cannot be located to testify.

Champmathieu pleads innocent to the charge of stealing, claiming that he found the apples on a broken branch on the ground. He emphatically denies that he is Jean Valjean or that he even knows Jean Valjean.

Brevet, the turnkey, positively identifies the prisoner as Jean Valjean as does Chenildieu, a convict for life, who claims they spent five years on the same chain gang. Cochepaille, also a convict for life, swears that the prisoner is Jean Valjean, also called "Jean-the-Jack, he was so strong."

The charges are proven; the prisoner will be found guilty. Just as the judge is about to pronounce sentence, a voice calls to the accusing witnesses. People in the court are stunned when they recognize Monsieur Madeleine.

Monsieur Madeleine's hair turns from gray to snowy white during the hour he has been watching the court proceedings. Instructing the jury to release the accused, Monsieur confesses that he is the real Jean Valjean and reveals that he has become an honest man. He proves that he is telling the truth by reminding Brevet of the checkered, knit suspenders he once wore when they were in the galleys together. He knows about the scar showing the letters T.F.P. which Chenildieu once burned into his left shoulder. He also knows about the date, March 1, 1815, the date the emperor landed in Cannes, burned with blue powder into Cochepaille's left arm. After finishing his testimony, Jean Valjean leaves the courtroom. It is so obvious that he is telling the truth that the defendant is immediately released.

Counter-Stroke

New Characters:

Sister Simplice, Sister Perpétue: *two nuns*

Summary

Fantine, who is gravely ill, believes that the mayor has gone to Montfermeil to fetch her child. Sister Simplice is nursing Fantine when the mayor arrives. He tells Sister that he will bring the child in two or three days. When she suggests that he not see Fantine so that they do not have to lie about the child, he insists that he must see her. Fantine is sleeping when he enters. Opening her eyes, she asks about Cosette.

The physician arrives and is informed of the situation. When Fantine asks about her child again, he lies to her, saying that although her daughter is near, her condition will worsen if she saw the child. He tells her she will see her daughter only when she is better. Although she does not believe seeing her child will cause any harm, Fantine agrees to wait, saying that she knows she will be happy. "All night, I saw figures in white, smiling on me." She hears a little girl laughing and playing in the courtyard below and assumes it is Cosette. Abruptly, she stops speaking and her face twists in terror. The mayor turns to see who is causing this rapid change in her expression. It is Javert.

He has come to arrest Jean Valjean. Fantine is astounded when Javert grabs the mayor by the collar. Since Javert will not speak to him in private, he has no choice but to ask to be free for three more days so he can go for the child. Fantine overhears. She realizes that they have lied to her and asks Monsieur the Mayor for her child. Javert interrupts, telling her the truth: that the mayor is really the convict, Jean Valjean. The others in the room hear the death rattle when Fantine, horrified once more, frantically tries to speak. Suddenly, she sinks back on the pillow. She is dead.

Jean Valjean rips an iron bar from the bed to use as a weapon. Warning Javert not to interfere, he goes to Fantine's bed. He gently arranges her hair and clothing and tenderly closes her eyes. Her face seems "strangely illumined" at that moment. "Death is the entrance into the great light." After gently kissing her hand, he gives himself up to Javert.

Jean is put in the city prison, and the news of his arrest causes a sensation. Only a few of the townspeople, including the old portress who had been his servant, continue to hold him in high regard. Sister Simplice and Sister Perpétue are in Monsieur Madeleine's home keeping watch over Fantine's corpse. The old portress goes through her usual nightly routine as if she is expecting Jean to return that night. She is surprised when he actually does arrive. He tells her that he has escaped by breaking one of the bars on the window. He sends her to find Sister Simplice and while she is gone, he writes a note identifying the 40-sous piece he stole from Petit Gervais and the ends of his "loaded club" which have been charred in the fire. He places them on the table with the note so they will be the first things seen when entering the room. He then tears up an old shirt and packs up his silver candlesticks. When Sister Simplice arrives, he hands her a note to give to Monsieur the Curé. He instructs Monsieur to take charge of his belongings, using some of his money to pay for the trial and giving the rest to the poor.

He barely finishes his instructions when they hear the old portress speaking to someone. It is Javert. Javert forces his way into the mayor's chamber, but all he finds is Sister Simplice on her knees, praying. When Javert asks her if she is alone, she lies and says she is. When he asks her if she has seen Jean Valjean, she lies again "as if she were adept" at it.

At the end of the chapter, the author makes a final comment about Fantine: "We all have but one mother — the earth. Fantine was restored to this mother."

Fantine

Analysis

When the story begins, the setting is a small town near the French Alps in 1815. It later moves to the village of Montefermeil. The author introduces Jean Valjean, the main character, as well as the primary social theme, which is society's treatment of the downtrodden. Jean is an outcast because he is a convict. The bishop, who becomes a symbol of salvation for Jean, is the only person who reaches out to him.

After an internal struggle with his own conscience, Jean accepts the bishop's invitation to forsake his evil ways and seek redemption. He becomes a respected citizen, makes his fortune, and does many good deeds. Twice his conscience is tested—once when he uses his great physical strength to save Fauchelevent and again when he must reveal his identity to save Champmathieu. In both instances, he unhesitatingly follows the path of goodness although he knows the price he must pay.

Two subplots are also introduced in this section. One revolves around the greedy Thénardiers who represent all of society's ills; the other involves Fantine, another lost soul, whose poverty forces hire strangers to care for her child while she searches for employment in another town.

Hugo makes frequent use of light images in this section. When Jean is at the bishop's, he is humbled by the sleeping bishop's radiance in the moonlight, a physical representation of the man's piety. Later, when Jean is caught stealing the bishop's silver candlesticks, the bishop responds by giving them to Jean. The candlesticks become one of Jean's most valued possessions, a symbol of the bishop's love, illuminating the path to goodness.

Fantine's face appears to be illuminated just after she dies, suggesting that in death she has found the peace that has eluded her throughout her sorrowful life. Cosette, Fantine's daughter, also suffers the hardships of poverty. The writer uses the image of a songless lark to suggest her fragile nature and the hopelessness of her condition.

Study Questions

1. How is a convict discriminated against after being released from prison?

2. What was Jean's crime? Why was he in prison so long?

3. What is Jean's moral dilemma the night he stays with the bishop?

4. What does the bishop do when Jean steals his silver?

5. Who is Petit Gervais?

6. Why does Fantine leave her child with the Thénardiers?

7. How does the author characterize the Thénardiers?

8. How does Jean make a fortune in M——sur M——?

9. How does Jean's rescue of Fauchelevant put him at risk?

10. Why does Jean risk revealing his true identity when Father Champmathieu is arrested?

Answers

1. Convicts are treated as second class citizens, and they are often paid lower wages. All doors are closed to them, and it is impossible for them to avoid being identified as convicts because they are forced to register with legal authorities wherever they go.

2. Jean was originally sentenced to five years in prison for stealing a loaf of bread. His sentence was eventually lengthened to a total of 19 years because of five failed escape attempts.

3. Jean wrestles with his conscience as he tries to decide whether or not to steal the bishop's silver. Although the bishop's treatment of him makes him feel guilty, he eventually succumbs to temptation.

4. The bishop forgives him and tells the police that the silver belongs to Jean, thus saving him from being returned to prison.

5. Petit Gervais is a young street musician from Savoy who meets Jean in the country. Jean steals money from him and later regrets it.

6. Fantine is poor and alone. She cannot care for her child because she must travel to another city to seek employment.

7. The Thénardiers are greedy and immoral. They are part of a "bastard class" who have none of the good qualities of the middle class and all of the faults of the lower class.

8. Jean makes a fortune by revolutionizing the manufacturing process of jet beads.

9. By using his Herculean strength to rescue Fauchelevent, Jean risks being recognized as a convict. When he was in prison, he gained a reputation for having extraordinary strength.

10. His conscience dictates that he must testify on Father Champmathieu's behalf because he knows that, unless he steps forward, the man will be judged guilty of crimes he did not commit.

Suggested Essay Topics

1. Discuss the internal struggle which haunts Jean after his release from prison. What forces influence the path he ultimately decides to travel?

2. Discuss the injustice of Jean Valjean's sentence. How does Victor Hugo use this character to protest the treatment of prisoners and convicts?

3. What social forces prompt Fantine to leave her child with the Thénardiers? Why does she think that she is doing the best possible thing for her child?

4. By the end of the first section, the reader develops a great deal of sympathy for Jean in spite of the fact that he is an ex-convict. How does the author use Jean's good deeds to develop him into a heroic character?

Cosette

The Ship Orion

Summary

Two newspaper articles record the recapture of Jean Valjean. The first, from *Drapeau Blanc*, July 25, 1823, notes the arrest of an individual known as Monsieur Madeleine who revitalized the jet and black glass industry with the invention of a new manufacturing process. Prior to his arrest, Valjean withdrew more than half a million francs, money which was honestly earned through his business, from Laffitte's Bank. Police were unable to determine where he had hidden the money. The second article appeared in the *Journal de Paris* on the same date. It reports that Jean Valjean had been appointed mayor and had established a profitable business under an assumed identity. After his arrest, he used his "Herculean strength" to escape. According to this account, during the three or four days before he was retaken, he withdrew "six or seven hundred francs" which were never recovered.

At his trial, Jean was found guilty of assault and robbery and condemned to death. Though he did not appeal to a higher court, the king "in his inexhaustible clemency, deigned to commute his sentence." Returned to the galleys at Toulon with a sentence of hard labor for life, Jean Valjean changes his number to 9430.

At the end of October 1823, the ship Orion sails into the harbor at Toulon. While the crew is furling the sail, the topman loses his balance. Grabbing the ropes as he plunges toward the sea, he hangs, helpless, swaying in the wind. No one dares to attempt to rescue him until a man clothed in the red garb of a convict scales the rigging and carries the sailor up to safety. Then the rescuer slides down the rigging to return to his work. Bystanders, unsure whether he loses his balance or is simply fatigued, watch in horror as the convict plunges into the sea between two ships. Though a search is mounted, the body is never recovered. The following morning, the Toulon Journal reports that the convict Jean Valjean has fallen into the sea and drowned.

Fulfilment of the Promise to the Departed

Summary

After throwing himself into the sea, Jean hides in a boat until evening and then swims to safety. He purchases new clothing and follows a circuitous route to Paris where he purchases a child's dress and finds lodging. He then goes to Montfermeil to rescue Cosette from the Thénardiers.

The Old Gorbeau House

New Character:

The Old Landlady: *runs Gorbeau House*

Summary

At the extreme edge of Paris there is a quarter known as the Horse Market. Within the crumbling walls of the quarter, far from the bustling neighborhoods of society, there is a small gabled cottage nearly hidden from view. The postal service refers to the house as No. 50-52, but it is known in the neighborhood as the Gorbeau House.

Jean Valjean carries the sleeping Cosette to the deserted Gorbeau House. It has been nine months since the death of her mother and Jean is ecstatic to have her with him. The noise of a wagon passing on the cobblestone street awakens the child. Slightly disoriented, she asks Jean for her broom and asks if she must sweep. He tells her she must play. Unquestioning, she spends a happy day with Jean and her doll.

Jean Valjean has been alone for 25 years. His sister and her children had disappeared, and in spite of a lengthy search, he has been unable to find them. He rescues the eight-year-old Cosette and feels the "grand emotion of a heart in its first love." His life takes another dramatic turn when, for the second time in his life, he sees a "white vision." "The bishop had caused the dawn of virtue on his horizon; Cosette evoked the dawn of love."

It is also Cosette's first experience with love. Separated early from her mother, she does not remember her. Since then, she has been neglected and abused. She loves Jean from the moment he rescues her and considers him handsome in spite of his 55 years.

Their hiding place is well-chosen. Only one window faces the boulevard. The upper floor is occupied by an old woman who works as their maid. Sometimes referred to as the landlady, she rented the garret to Jean on Christmas Day. Jean pretends to be a wealthy gentleman who has lost most of his money. He tells her Cosette is his granddaughter.

In these poor surroundings, they live happily. Jean, who learned to read in the galleys for the purpose of evil, now teaches Cosette to read and to spell and to pray. She loves him and calls him Father. He grows stronger while protecting and nurturing her.

Jean never went out during the day, but in the early hours of the evening he strolled along the side streets, often with Cosette. His shabby clothes make others think he is a beggar. Because he sometimes gives money to beggars, people in the quarter refer to him as "the beggar who gives alms."

The old landlady, a "crabbed creature," is suspicious. She questions Cosette who knows nothing. One day, through a chink in the door, she observes Jean as he rips open the lining of his lapel and removes a 1000-franc bill. When he later asks her to get it changed for him, he tells her that it is from the interest on his property.

Jean never passes the beggar in Saint Medard without giving him money. One evening as he and Cosette pass, Jean stops to put money in his hand. Their eyes meet. Though the beggar looks no different, Jean recoils in terror. He thinks he has seen Javert.

Days later, as he is giving Cosette a spelling lesson, he sees a ray of light through the keyhole in his room. Someone is listening through the door; but when the light disappears, there is no sound of footsteps. The following morning, awakened by a creaking door in the hall, he looks through the keyhole and observes a tall man passing his room. The light from the window illuminates a man wearing a long frock-coat and carrying a short club. It is Javert.

Jean inquires about the stranger in the house and the landlady tells him that the gentleman, M. Daumont, is a new tenant. When the old woman leaves, he gathers 100 francs. Jean drops a five-franc piece and it rolls across the floor. At dusk, when the street appears to be deserted, Jean and Cosette leave Gorbeau House. The author notes that "there might have been someone hidden behind a tree."

A Dark Chase Needs A Silent Hound

Summary

The street called Rue Droit Mur is lined with poor houses on one side and several buildings of one or two stories on the other. At the corner, the wall on one side of the street is very low. A lime-tree grows above it. The wall seems to surround a garden, so Jean tries to open one of the doors. Unable to budge it, he tries to open another and discovers that it merely appears to be a door. When he tears off a board, there is a wall behind it.

Hearing noises, he looks around the corner and sees seven or eight soldiers, led by Javert, coming towards him. His greatest fear of returning to the galleys is the fear of losing Cosette. He knows he can scale the 18-foot wall to get into the garden, but he needs a rope to lift Cosette.

Remembering that the street lamps in Paris are raised and lowered for lighting by a rope, an idea comes to Jean. He cuts a rope from the nearest lamp, ties it around Cosette, scales the wall, and then hoists her up. No sooner do they reach the top than they hear Javert and his soldiers on the street below. Carrying Cosette, he climbs down the lime-tree into the garden.

Though the building is in ruins, Jean finds a room which is used as a shed and takes Cosette into it. He hears the voice of Javert and

the sounds of the patrol searching for them and puts his hand on Cosette's mouth. He does not breathe. When the noise fades, he is calmed by the celestial sound of the voices of women and children coming from a dilapidated building overlooking the garden. It is like a choir of angels that makes both of them feel they should be on their knees. After a while, the chant ceases and it is silent.

Between one and two o'clock in the morning, Cosette awakes. The shed is open on all sides, and the cold wind and damp ground make her tremble. Jean wraps her in his coat.

Cosette falls asleep and Jean contemplates the situation. He decides that as long as he has her, he needs nothing else. Hearing the sound of a tinkling bell, he turns to see someone else in the garden. The person appears to walk with a limp as he goes from one patch of melons to the next. Terrified, Jean picks up Cosette and moves to the farthest corner of the shed where he continues to watch the man whose every movement, makes the bell tinkle. Jean feels Cosette's cold hands. When he is unable to awaken her, he realizes he must find a warm place for her immediately.

Jean approaches the man in the garden and offers him a hundred francs for shelter for the night. The full moon illuminates Jean's face, allowing the man to recognize him. The old man is astonished to see Father Madeleine in such mean circumstances. He tells Jean that he is Fauchelevent whose life Jean once saved. Jean has inadvertently stumbled into the garden of the Convent of Petit Picpus where the old man works as a gardener. He is covering his melons to protect them from frost. Since no men are allowed in the convent, he must wear a bell to warn the young girls in the convent that he is coming so they can avoid him. Fauchelevant has three rooms in a shanty in a corner of the convent where he takes Cosette and Jean to warm by the fire.

Cemeteries Take What Is Given Them

New Characters:

The Prioress and The Reverend Mother: *nuns at the Convent of the Petit Picpus*

Summary

The convent is a safe place for them to hide because no one would think to look for them there. It is a also a dangerous place because no men are allowed, and it is a crime for Jean to be there. Fauchelevant resolves to devote himself to Jean.

Fauchelevent, Jean Valjean, and Cosette visit the prioress and the reverend mother. They tell the reverend mother that Jean is Ultimus, the brother of Fauchelevent, and that Cosette is his granddaughter. The prioress remarks, "She will be homely." Perhaps because of her comment, the reverend mother agrees to admit Cosette to the convent school as a charity case and allow Ultimus to stay as an assistant gardener. The following day, two bells are heard tinkling in the garden.

Cosette adjusts to life in the convent school, and Jean uses the skills he learned as a pruner to improve the orchard. He is content living in the convent because Cosette visits him for an hour every day, and he can watch her while she plays. Several years pass.

Cosette

Analysis

The time is 1823. The setting changes to Paris, where the rest of the novel takes place. Readers should note that the city of Paris is divided into four parts known as quarters. The Seine River flows through the city, splitting it into two parts, the left bank and the right bank.

Twice in this part of the novel Jean uses his great strength to escape. He uses it to fake his own death, and later depends on it again when he is on the run with Cosette from Javert and his men. Throughout the novel the author parallels the physical strength Jean needs to survive with the spiritual strength he requires to follow his conscience.

The use of the color white comes into play as an image when Cosette is referred to as a "white vision." Like the bishop, she illuminates his life by offering him something good. For the first time in his life he has someone to love and is no longer alone. She becomes the central focus of his entire life.

Bird imagery is used once again when Jean and Cosette are compared to the owl and the wren, images suggesting his wisdom and her helplessness. The "nest" they create at Gorbeau House symbolizes safety and comfort for both of them. When they are forced to flee, they find refuge in a convent as if they are being sheltered by the arms of God.

Study Questions

1. Why does Jean return to prison? What is he convicted of and what is his sentence?

2. How does Jean escape?

3. How does Jean fulfill a promise to Fantine?

4. What does Cosette give Jean that he has never had before?

5. In the first section of the book, the author compares Fantine to a lark. What bird images does he use in the second section?

6. Why do people refer to Jean as the "beggar who gives alms"?

7. Why does Jean abruptly leave Gorbeau House?

8. What is Jean's greatest fear in being recaptured?

9. How does Jean escape from Javert and his men?

10. How do Jean and Fauchelevant convince the prioress and the reverend mother to allow Jean and Cosette to stay at the convent?

Answers

1. Jean reveals his identity when he testifies at Father Champmathieu's trial. He is found guilty of assault and robbery and condemned to death. His sentence is later commuted to hard labor for life.

2. After climbing a rigging to save a sailor who has lost his balance, Jean plunges into the sea and is presumed to have drowned.

3. He rescues Cosette from the Thénardiers.

4. For the first time in his life, Jean has someone to love.

5. Jean and Cosette are referred to as the owl and the wren when they find refuge in Gorbeau House. Jean is wise, and Cosette is small and helpless like a little wren. Gorbeau House becomes their nest, a place of safety and solace.

6. Jean's shabby appearance makes him look like a beggar, but he always gives money to the beggars he passes on the street.

7. He leaves to escape from Javert, who has moved into Gorbeau House.

8. Jean's greatest fear is losing Cosette.

9. He escapes by scaling a garden wall and using the rope from a streetlight to hoist Cosette over the wall of the convent.

10. They say that Jean is Fauchelevent's brother, who has come with his granddaughter to visit. Saying they have no money, they convince the prioress and the reverend mother to admit Cosette to the convent school as a charity case.

Suggested Essay Topics

1. Discuss the ways in which Jean depends on his great physical strength to help him escape from the Orion and from Javert.

2. Javert is primarily a symbol of law and order. Contrast the author's development of this character with his development of the character Jean Valjean.

3. Comment on the settings the author uses in this section of the novel. How are they used to contribute both to the development of the characters and the advancement of the plot?

4. Discuss the relationship that develops between Cosette and Jean Valjean. What fulfillment does each find in the relationship, and why is Jean willing to risk his freedom for it?

Marius

The Grand Bourgeois

New Characters:

M. Gillenormand: *an elderly bourgeois gentleman*

Mademoiselle Gillenormand the Elder: *oldest daughter of Gillenormand*

Lieutenant Théodule Gillenormand: *Mademoiselle's nephew*

Summary

M. Gillenormand is 90 years old. He treats his 50-year-old daughter like a child and sometimes beats his domestics. He is "truly a man of another age — the genuine bourgeois of the eighteenth century, a very perfect specimen, a little haughty."

Gillenormand's daughters are ten years apart in age. The younger daughter is happy, gay, and married to the man of her dreams. The other, Mademoiselle the elder, remains unmarried. Ever modest, she is called the Prude and allows only her nephew Théodule to kiss her. She is a religious woman "of the fraternity of the Virgin" who keeps the house for her father and his grandson. The boy is terribly afraid of his grandfather.

The Grandfather and the Grandson

New Characters:

George Pontmercy: *soldier married to Gillenormand's younger daughter*

Marius: *son of Pontmercy and grandson of Gillenormand*

Abbé Mabeuf: *the priest who is curé of Vernon*

Summary

It is about 1817 in the town of Vernon. George Pontmercy lives in a small, humble house with a woman who waits on him. He is about fifty, has white hair and a scar that extends from his forehead across his cheek. He was young soldier when the revolution broke out. With his regiment, he fought on almost every front from Italy to Turkey to Germany. The emperor awarded him the cross. He was a brave and distinguished soldier and an outstanding officer who was wounded several times. He fought with Napoleon at Waterloo. There, he was wounded again by a saber across the cheek when he rescued the colors from the opposition. Covered with blood, he delivered them to the emperor, who praised and thanked him.

During the Restoration, Pontmercy was reduced to half-pay and sent to live in a government residence in Vernon. Louis XVIII, ignoring Pontmercy's valiant efforts in the campaign, "recognized neither his position of officer of the Legion of Honor, nor his rank of colonel, nor his title of baron." He continues to use the title Colonel Baron Pontmercy and wears the rosette of an officer every time he goes out in spite of warnings from the government that this is illegal. He responds by asking if he is still permitted to wear his scar.

Between two wars, Pontmercy had married Mademoiselle Gillenormand who died in 1815 leaving a son. Her father, M. Gillenormand, considered his son-in-law "a blockhead" and demanded that his grandson live with him. Because the old man threatened to disinherit the boy if he did not have his way, Pontmercy gave in and agreed not to see or speak to his son Marius, thus insuring a large inheritance from his Aunt Gillenormand. Influenced by the grandfather, Marius gradually became ashamed of his father.

Every few months, Pontmercy would travel to Paris. He would go to Saint Sulpice, where he would hide behind a pillar so he could see Marius when the aunt took him to mass. There he met Abbé Mabeuf, the curé of Vernon, whose brother was a warden at Saint Sulpice. One day when the priest was visiting his brother, he saw Pontmercy and recognized him as the man he had seen hiding behind the pillar with tears in his eyes. The two brothers visited the colonel and eventually learned the whole story.

The father's only contact with his son was letters, dictated by the aunt, which he received on January 1 and on St. George's Day. The colonel's replies were kept by the grandfather and never read.

In 1827, when Marius has just turned 18, his grandfather sends him to Vernon to see his father who is ill and asking for his son. Marius is convinced that his father does not love him and is therefore reluctant to go. Raised to be politically sympathetic with the Restoration, he does not recognize his father's title as baron or colonel.

The colonel dies of a brain fever the same evening Marius arrives in Vernon. Marius has no feelings when he looks at the corpse of the father he is now seeing for the first and last time. The colonel leaves nothing except a piece of paper on which he has written the story of a sergeant named Thénardier who saved his life at the Battle of Waterloo. He requests that his son do all he can for Thénardier if they ever meet. Marius stays in Vernon for two days, long enough to bury his father, and then returns to Paris. He wears crepe on his hat as a sign of mourning. Otherwise, his father is forgotten.

One Sunday when Marius goes to mass at Saint Sulpice, he inadvertently sits in a chair which has the name Monsieur Mabeuf, church-warden, written on the back of it. An old man approaches him and says, " Monsieur, this is my place." After mass, the old man approaches Marius again to explain that for ten years he has observed a man who attended mass every two or three months just to see his son. Mabeuf explains that this was the only time the man could see the child he loved so much because the other relatives would disinherit the boy if he attempted to make contact with him. The father, one of Bonaparte's colonels, had "sacrificed himself that his son might some day be rich and happy." He tells Marius that the man's name was Pontmercy, and Marius realizes that it is his father he is hearing about and that his father really did love him.

The next day Marius asks his grandfather if he can be away for three days to go on a hunting expedition with friends. The grandfather mistakenly assumes that he is having a love affair and tells him to take four days.

When Marius returns from his travels, he goes to the law library where he devours volumes of history books about the republic and the empire. The more he reads, the more he changes his political opinions. By the time he finishes, he has shed his royalist views, becoming a revolutionary and learning to admire his father. He even orders a hundred cards with his name, Baron Marius Pontmercy, engraved on them. Occasionally he travels to Montfermeil to search for Thénardier. His grandfather thinks he is "going astray."

The grand-nephew of M. Gillenormand is a handsome military officer named Lieutenant Théodule Gillenormand. He visits the old gentleman so seldom that Marius has never seen him. One day he stops to visit his aunt when he is on his way to a new post. She gives him some money and invites him to stay for at least a week. Though he cannot stay, he informs her that his cousin Marius is booked on the same coach. Influenced by the money she has given him, he agrees to spy on Marius.

That evening, when they are on the coach, Théodule observes Marius buying flowers. Later, he follows Marius to a church, assuming that he is on his way to a meet a woman. However, Marius goes behind the building where Théodule watches him, crying, as he scatters the flowers on his father's grave.

Marius returns on the evening of the third day. He decides to go swimming for some exercise but stops in his room briefly to take off his coat and the black ribbon he wears around his neck. After he leaves, his grandfather and aunt go into his room. The grandfather opens the black leather box which hangs from the black ribbon. He expects to see a portrait of a young lady and is surprised to find instead a note written to Marius by his father as well as the hundred cards Marius had printed with his true name on them.

Just then Marius returns. His grandfather asks him what this means. He replies by recounting his father's brave deeds and telling how much he now reveres his father. An argument over politics ensues and Marius is ordered out of the house. The following day Gillenormand instructs his daughter to send Marius a small sum of money each month and to never speak of him again.

In the confusion of Marius' departure, the black medallion containing his father's will is lost. Marius is convinced that his grandfather has destroyed it. He leaves with only a few clothes and 30 francs and has no idea where he is going.

The Excellence of Misfortune

New Character:

Courfeyrac: *a friend of Marius*

Summary

Marius is very poor. Even still, he returns the money his aunt sends each month and tells her he does not need anything. He continues to wear black clothes in mourning for his father. When they get shabby, he only goes out at night. He lives with his friend Courfeyrac, whose small collection of law books helps him satisfy the requirement of a law library for admission to the bar. When he is admitted to the bar, he sends his grandfather a formal but cold letter to inform him. M. Gillenormand reads it and rips it to pieces.

Courfeyrac introduces Marius to a friend in the publishing business where Marius gets a job in the literary department. Among other tasks, he translates works, compiles bibliographies, and writes prospectuses for 700 francs per year. Though it is not very much, he carefully manages his money and never gives up hope. He continues to search for Thénardier but learns only that the bankrupt innkeeper has disappeared.

Now 20 years old, he has not seen his grandfather in three years.

He does not know how much the old man loves him.

In mid-1831, the old woman who serves Marius informs him that his neighbors, the Jondrette family, will be evicted for not paying their rent. They owe 20 francs for six months' rent. Marius has only 30 francs, but he gives her 25 for the family and instructions not to tell them it is from him.

The Conjunction of Two Stars

Summary

By now Marius is a handsome young man with jet black hair. Girls are attracted to him, but he thinks they stare at him because of his worn out clothes so he becomes a loner. Though he especially avoids women, there are two he never shies away from. One is the old woman who sweeps his room; the other is a girl he sees in the Luxembourg Gardens. Each day she and a gentleman of about 60 walk in the park and rest on the same bench. She is about 13 or 14 when Marius first sees her. He watches her for about a year.

Marius is in the habit of parading back and forth past their bench, but he has never spoken to them. Others, including his friend Confreyac, notice the pair, but Confreyac thinks the girl is homely so he nicknames them Mademoiselle Lenoire (black) and Monsieur Leblanc (white), referring to the color of her dress and his white hair.

For six months Marius does not go to the park. One summer day he returns to find the gentleman and the girl on the same bench. The man looks the same, but the girl, now 15, has become "a noble, beautiful creature, with all the most bewitching outlines of a woman." He resumes his daily walks in the park.

One day as Marius passes, the girl looks up and their eyes meet briefly. When he returns home that night, he looks in the mirror and notices for the first time how shabby he looks.

The following day Marius wears his new coat, pants, boots, and hat to the park. He passes the bench where the girl is sitting and then takes a seat near her, glancing at her frequently. After about 15 minutes, he goes home. That night he forgets to eat dinner but

carefully brushes his clothes before going to bed.

The next day Ma'am Bougon, the old portress who has been given the nickname by Courfeyrac, is surprised to see Marius go out in his new clothes again. She tries to follow him but her asthma prevents her from keeping up with him and she loses him. For the next two weeks, Marius goes to the park every day, not to walk, but to sit in the same place, though he does not understand why.

At the end of the second week, Marius is sitting on the bench holding an open book. He has not turned a page for two hours. The girl looks at him as she and her companion pass, and Marius feels like "his brain is on fire." He is in love for the first time.

For the next month, Marius visits the park every day. Though he tries not to attract the father's attention, he boldly positions himself where the girl will see him the most. Eventually, the father begins to vary his schedule and sometimes visits the park alone. One evening, Marius find a white handkerchief with the initials U.F. on the bench the old man and the girl have just left. Assuming that the handkerchief belongs to the girl, Marius guesses that her first name is Ursula. He kisses the handkerchief, holds it over his heart, and goes to sleep that night with it pressed to his lips. Actually, the handkerchief has fallen from the old man's pocket.

Wanting to know more about her, Marius follows her to her modest home in the Rue de l'Oest. One night he asks the porter about them and learns that they live on the third floor and that the gentleman, who lives on his income, does a lot of good works for the poor. The following day, Marius again follows them. After his daughter is inside, the old man turns and looks at Marius. After that, they no longer go to the park. Marius watches their window every evening but does not see them. On the eighth day, the window is dark. The porter informs Marius that they have moved.

The Noxious Poor

Summary

Marius searches for the girl and her father but does not find them. Depressed, he reproaches himself for following them. One day he sees a man who is dressed like a laborer. Beneath his cap, Marius sees a few strands of white hair. Though he thinks he recognizes M. Leblanc, he cannot understand why he would be dressed as a laborer.

A young girl visits Marius one evening and delivers a letter signed by his neighbor, Jondrette. The letter thanks Marius for the kindness he showed by paying the rent six months before and explains that the family has no money for food and asks Marius to help them again. While Marius reads the letter, Jondrette's daughter, who is wearing such tattered clothes that they barely cling to her body, snoops around his room moving things and inspecting everything. She mentions that her father served in the army and fought at Waterloo. She also tells Marius that she has seen him visiting Father Mabeuf. Marius has only five francs and 16 sous. He gives her the five francs and keeps the 16 sous for his own dinner.

Though Marius has been poor for the past five years, he has not known real misery. He has just seen real misery in the form of Jondrette's daughter. "In fact, he who has seen the misery of man only has seen nothing, he must see the misery of woman; he who has seen the misery of woman only has seen nothing, he must see the misery of childhood." Marius feels guilty for ignoring the plight of his neighbors who are separated from him by only by a thin plaster wall. He thinks their wretched behavior is caused by their circumstances. "There is a point, moreover, at which the unfortunate and the infamous are associated and confounded in a single word, a fatal word, "*Les Misérables...*" Marius finds a hole in the wall near the ceiling. Standing on his bureau, he can see into the Jondrette's apartment.

Peering through the hole, Marius sees the daughter who is now wearing an old gown. She did not have it on when she visited his room, perhaps so that she would look more pitiful. She excitedly announces that the philanthropist will be arriving any moment in a coach. The father orders the family to put out the fire and break a pane of glass, and he puts his foot through the bottom of the chair. The younger daughter cuts her hand when she breaks the window so the father rips up the shirt he is wearing and wraps it, pronouncing that they are now ready to receive the philanthropist.

There is a knock at the door; an old man and a girl enter the Jondrettes' room. Marius, still watching through the hole in the wall, is astounded to see that it is Monsieur Leblanc and his daughter. The daughter places a package on the table.

Jondrette thanks his visitors for the blankets and clothing in the package. Seeking sympathy, he tells them that they have no food and no fire, that their only chair is broken, and that the window is broken. He lies when he says that his daughter has injured her arm working in a factory. His wife, he says, is ill. He again lies when he says that they will be evicted the following day because they owe the landlord 40 francs unpaid rent for an entire year. In fact, Marius had paid for half a year.

M. Leblanc gives him five francs, all he has, and promises to return at six o'clock with 60 francs. He also leaves his coat for Jondrette, who puts it on immediately.

Near six o'clock, Marius again looks through the hole in the wall and observe a charcoal furnace in the fireplace. A chisel lying in the coals is red hot. Near the door are a pile of ropes and a pile of old iron. The Jondrette apartment is a perfect place for crime as it is "the most retired room of the most isolated house of the most solitary boulevard in Paris."

Jondrette tells his wife that they must have two chairs, and she quickly responds that she will borrow them from the neighbor. Before he can move, she enters Marius' room and takes two chairs. She does not see Marius who is concealed by a shadow. She returns to her apartment, and her husband places one chair on each side of the table and puts a screen in front of the fireplace to hide the furnace. Marius now realizes that the rope in the corner is actually a rope ladder, and the pile of iron is a pile of large iron tools. Jondrette takes a large carving knife out of the table drawer, tests the blade, and replaces it in the drawer. Marius, observing all this, takes out his pistol and cocks it.

Precisely at six o'clock, Jondrette puts out the candle and M. Leblanc enters. He puts four louis on the table. While he is thanking M. Leblanc, Jondrette tells his wife to send the carriage away. She quietly leaves the room as her husband offers their visitor a chair. She returns moments later and whispers that the carriage is gone. Jondrette sits in the other chair, facing his visitor.

M. Leblanc inquires about the daughter's injury and comments that the wife looks better. Jondrette tells him that she is dying. While they are talking, Marius sees a man noiselessly enter the back of the room. The intruder has tattooed arms and his face is blackened. He sits on the bed and stays behind the wife.

M. Leblanc instinctively turns toward the stranger and asks who he is. Jondrette explains that he is a neighbor and distracts Leblanc with conversation about a picture he wants to sell. Another man with a blackened face silently enters and sits on the bed Jondrette tells Leblanc to ignore him. While Jondrette continues to talk about his painting, two more men with blackened faces and

bare arms enter the room. Leblanc stares at them. Jondrette explains that their faces are dark because they are chimney sweeps who work with charcoal. When he asks Leblanc how much he will pay for the painting, Leblanc says that it is only a tavern sign worth a few francs. Jondrette asks for a thousand crowns. (It is the sign the Thénardiers had above the door of their inn in Montfermeil.)

Leblanc stands with his back to the wall watching Jondrette the whole time. Jondrette becomes more and more angry. He is

like a mad man. Suddenly, he moves toward Leblanc and shouts, "...Do you know me?"

The apartment door suddenly flies open. Three men wearing blue shirts and paper masks enter. One is armed with a club, another holds an ax, and the third carries a key from a prison door. As if he were awaiting their arrival, Jondrette angrily repeats his question. When Leblanc declares that he does not know who he is, Jondrette, crazed, declares that he is Thénardier, the innkeeper of Montfermeil, but Leblanc still does not know who he is.

Marius, still watching from the other side of the wall, is com-

pletely unnerved when he hears the name Thénardier. Remembering his father's will, he is astounded that Thénardier is a monster
about to commit a crime. He hesitates, knowing that he must act if
he is to save M. Leblanc.

In the meantime, Thénardier, still in a frenzy, accuses Leblanc
of being a thoughtless millionaire who preys on the poor. He identifies him as the one who took Fantine's child away. Leblanc seizes
the moment when Thénardier turns his back and springs toward
the window. He is half out when the three black-faced men drag
him back into the room and throw him down. Thénardier's wife
grabs his hair, and one of the men raises a club to hit him on the
head. Marius, still watching, is about to shoot when Thénardier
instructs his men not to hurt Leblanc.

Leblanc puts up a struggle, crushing two of the men and knock-
ing over Thénardier, but the others subdue him, and he stops re-
sisting. They tie him to the foot of the bed and search him, finding
only six francs. Thénardier, whose demeanor has changed from
violent to calm, sits near him and quietly begins to talk. He informs
his captive that he wants 200,000 francs. He unties one hand and
forces Leblanc to write: "Come immediately, I have imperative need
of you. The person who will give you this note is directed to bring
you to me. I am waiting for you."

Thénardier asks his name, and he says it is Urbain Fabre. Finding the initials U.F. on the handkerchief he has taken from his prisoner, Thénardier instructs him to sign the note with the initials and
address it to his daughter, Mademoiselle Fabre. He then gives the
note to his wife and tells her to deliver it right away.

They wait. When the wife returns, she tells them it was the
wrong address. Thénardier, furious, asks his prisoner why he used
a false address. He says he did it to gain time. With only one leg
tied to the bed, Leblanc has loosened his bonds. Before anyone
can react, he springs free and grabs the hot chisel from the fire. He
proclaims that they cannot make him do what he does not want to
do or write what he doesn't want to write. Rolling up his sleeve, he
puts the glowing chisel on his left arm. Marius is horrified, and even
the criminals wince when they hear his flesh sizzle. Leblanc throws
the chisel out the window and tells them to do what they want with
him. Taking the knife from the drawer, Thénardier suggests they
kill him.

Marius, hoping to save both the victim and his persecutor, wraps a chunk of plaster with a note written by Thénardier's daughters which says, "THE COGNES (Police) ARE HERE." He hurls it into his neighbor's apartment. Thénardier, recognizing Eponine's writing, rushes to escape through the window. The others want to go first so they decide to draw lots. From the doorway, someone asks if they would like to use his hat to draw the lots. It is Javert.

Javert had posted his men in front of the building at nightfall. After recognizing some of the bandits and seeing the coach come and go, he decided to go up. His men handcuff everyone and untie Leblanc. Javert sits at the table, starts to write something, and then calls for the gentleman who had been tied up. However, the prisoner of the bandits has disappeared in the confusion.

Marius

Analysis

This portion of the novel, which begins in 1831, introduces additional characters and subplots and advances the story of Jean and Cosette. One new subplot revolves around Marius and his family and their opposing political views. Another concerns the development of a love relationship between Marius and Cosette.

The author develops the theme of the old vs. the new social order, the bourgeois vs. the revolutionary, by contrasting M. Gillenormand and George Pontmercy. Gillenormand, the bourgeois gentleman, symbolizes the old order. His rough treatment of his daughter and servants and his interference in the relationship between Marius and his father make Gillenormand the villain. In contrast, Pontmercy is a military hero whose bravery is well documented. He represents the revolutionists and forces of change that were sweeping across France. A description of the relationship between Pontmercy and Thénardier foreshadows events which will occur later in the novel.

Further social commentary is offered and the title of the novel is explained by the discussion of misery in this section. The Jondrettes, though vile and miserable people, are no less miserable than the merely unfortunate characters. As the author points out, few people who are reduced to poverty and mean circumstances remain pure.

A Biblical reference to Judas, who betrayed Jesus, foreshadows the betrayal of M. Leblanc by the Jondrettes. Throughout this section Jean is called M. Leblanc because of his white hair, perhaps suggesting that he is an intrinsically good man. In the Jondrettes' apartment, the forces of evil, represented by the men with blackened faces, gather against him. He resists by lying to them and declares his independence by branding his own arm with a hot chisel, indicating his ability to resist evil.

Study Questions

1. What kind of man is M. Gillenormand?

2. What were the highlights of Pontmercy's military career?

3. Why does Marius live with his grandfather instead of his father?

4. What instruction does Pontmercy leave Marius when he dies?

5. How does the information Monsieur Mabeuf gives Marius change his mind about his father and about politics?

6. When Marius falls in love, how does he inadvertently change her life?

7. What lies do the Jondrettes tell to gain sympathy and assistance from M. Leblanc and his daughter?

8. What is Jondrette's real identity, and why does he hate M. Leblanc?

9. Why does Marius not act immediately to save Leblanc and his daughter?

10. How does the appearance of Javert abort Jondrette's plan?

Answers

1. M. Gillenormand is a bourgeois man who is somewhat of a snob. He wants to control everyone in his life, and when they do not do what he wants, he punishes them. He rejects the

husband of his daughter for political reasons, prevents Marius from living with his father, beats his servants, and treats his 50-year-old daughter like a child. He banishes Marius from his house when Marius disagrees with him.

2. He was a decorated soldier of the revolution who fought in almost every campaign including Waterloo.

3. M. Gillenormand has threatened to disinherit Marius unless the boy lives with him.

4. He asks his son to do all he can for Thénardier, who saved his life at the Battle of Waterloo.

5. Monsieur Mabeuf tells Marius that his father loved him very much and that he attended mass just to get a glimpse of his son. He informs Marius of the fact that his father made this sacrifice so that he would not be disinherited by his grandfather. Realizing for the first time that his father loves him, Marius is compelled to learn more about his father's political views. After much research, he changes his own political views and becomes a revolutionary.

6. Marius follows her to her home and makes inquiries about her. This makes Jean nervous so he decides to move to another location.

7. Jondrette says that his family will be evicted because he owes the landlord rent for an entire year when, in fact, Marius has paid for half a year. He also lies when he claims that his wife is ill and that his daughter has injured her arm in a factory. He says they have no food, no fire, and that the window and their only chair are broken. The truth is that he put out the fire and intentionally broke the window and the chair.

8. Jondrette is really Thénardier, who he hates Leblanc for taking Cosette away and depriving him of the money Fantine paid him.

9. Although Marius has a gun, he hesitates to use it when he learns that Jondrette is really Thénardier, the man who rescued his father. Hoping to save all of them by breaking up the situation, he throws a piece of plaster into the apartment

with a note attached to it. The note says that the police have arrived.

10. Javert and his men rush into the apartment, handcuff everyone, and untie M. Leblanc. In the confusion, he escapes.

Suggested Essay Topics

1. M. Gillenormand is a bourgeois gentleman and a royalist. His son-in-law, George Pontmercy, is a military hero and a revolutionary. Discuss the political differences which separate M. Gillenormand and George Pontmercy and the ways in which these differences affect the way they treat each other and other people.

2. Discuss the title of the novel, and show how Hugo has created characters to support his definition of misery. Comment on the characters he creates to represent various human conditions of misery.

3. Discuss the underhanded ways in which members of the Gillenormand family strive to maintain control over Marius and deprive him of a relationship with his father.

4. How does Marius change in this portion of the novel? What steps does he take toward his own independence?

5. What good deeds does Marius do which cause the reader to think of him as an honorable man? How do these compare with the good deeds of Jean Valjean?

SECTION FIVE

St. Denis

Eponine

Summary

Marius, having watched the entire scene, leaves the house just after Javert and goes to Courfeyrac's. Courfeyrac has moved from the Left Bank to the Rue de la Verrerie, a neighborhood where there are more revolutionists. The following morning, Marius returns home, pays his rent, and leaves without leaving a forwarding address. Ma'am Bougon thinks he is involved with the criminals who were arrested the previous night. Marius leaves for two reasons. One is that it is the place where he first encountered "a social deformity perhaps more hideous than the evil rich man: the evil poor." The other is that he does not want to be involved in a trial. He does not want to have to testify against Thénardier.

He is unhappy because he now realizes that he doesn't even know the name of the girl he loves. Finally, he is once again poor because he has stopped working and "nothing is more dangerous than discontinued labor; it is a habit lost. A habit easy to abandon, difficult to resume."

Marius does not stay with Courfeyrac. Rather, he lives on the Boulevard de la Sante, the seventh tree down from the Rue Croulebarbe. He sits on the bank of a brook, frozen in a state of inaction. He is sad, and his idle state makes the loss of the girl even more difficult to bear. He watches the women washing clothes and notices the birds singing and is pleased by the happy sounds they make.

He is approached by Eponine who, despite the fact that her clothes are dirtier and more ragged than ever, looks beautiful. She tells him that she has been in jail and has been looking for him for six weeks since she was released. She offers to mend his shirt and tells him that she can make him happy. She reveals that she has the address of the young lady Marius is missing. Of course, he is thrilled and asks her to take him there. She agrees to lead him but warns him not to follow her too closely because it would not be good for him to be seen in public with a woman like her.

The House in the Rue Plumet

New Character:

Touissant: *the servant of Jean and Cosette*

Summary

Jean Valjean, Cosette, and a servant named Toussaint, an old woman Jean rescued from a hospital, live in a small house on a deserted street in Saint Germain. Built as a summer house by the president of the Parlement of Paris the century before, it has an acre of land and a huge iron gate which faces the street. At the rear of the property is a small building with only two rooms and a cellar which was originally built to hide a child and a nurse. It has a secret passage which leads to a building about a third of a mile away. Jean rented the property in October 1829 and had the secret passage restored.

Though Jean was happy in the convent, he left after Old Fauchelevent died because he felt that Cosette should have the chance to have a more normal life. He told the reverend prioress that he had received a small inheritance and gave her 5000 francs for the five years Cosette had spent there.

When they leave the convent, he takes with him the little box Cosette refers to as "the inseparable." He always carries the key with him and from then on always has the box with him. He uses the name Ultimus Fauchelevent. Afraid now to go out in public, Jean also rents two other properties in distant quarters of the city in case he needs to change his address quickly.

Cosette and the servant live in the main house, and Jean lives a spartan life in a cottage in the back yard although he does eat with Cosette. Each day they go for a walk in a remote part of the Luxembourg, and every Sunday they go to church.

The mail they receive is tax bills and notices from the National Guard addressed to M. Fauchelevent. Jean would put on a uniform several times a year and perform his guard duties. He does this willingly because it provides a good disguise. At 60, he could have been legally exempt, but he looks like a man in his fifties and welcomes the opportunity to be a part of society and still hide his identity.

All three occupants of the cottage enter through the secret passage, and Jean allows the garden to be overgrown so that it does not attract attention. His precautions may have given him a false sense of security.

Cosette is only 14 years old when she leaves the convent. She has received a fine formal education there, but she is very naive about life because she has no mother. Life in the house on the Rue Plumet is also solitary, but it offers the promise of freedom.

She has only vague memories of her mother, but she does remember her horrid life with the Thénardiers from whom she was rescued by Jean. She loved him passionately as a daughter and felt that "her mother's soul had passed into this good man." She is proud and happy to be with Jean, and he thanks God for her love.

Cosette had often been told that she was homely so she thought of herself as unattractive even though Jean told her she was not. Once while they were still at the convent, she was surprised by the way he looked at her. Another time when she was walking on the street, she heard someone behind her say she was pretty but not well dressed. Finally, one day she is shocked to overhear old Toussaint remark to Jean that she is so pretty. Cosette runs to her room and looks in the mirror, amazed to find that she is beautiful.

Jean was aware of her beauty long before she was. It causes him anguish because he knows that one day she will find a husband and leave him. Cosette, once aware of her looks, resolves to look good. Within a month she is one of the best dressed women in the city. Six months later, Marius sees her again in the park.

Marius and Cosette continue to see each other in the park. Their attraction for one another grows, despite the fact that they do not speak to one another. Each adores the other from afar and looks forward to their daily encounters.

Marius tries not to bring himself to the attention of her father, but Jean is very aware of the young man. He notices that Marius dresses better, pretends to read while he is sitting in the park, and no longer approaches them. Jean despises the young man. One day, unable to control himself, Jean makes a negative comment about Marius. Cosette responds by saying that she thinks he is charming. Another day, after they had been sitting in the park for three hours, Cosette surprised him by not wanting to leave so soon.

Though he thought he was no longer capable of evil thoughts, Jean's dislike of the young man grows, and he glares at Marius. When the porter informs him that Marius has been asking about them, Jean changes their residence within a week and resolves to never set foot in the Luxembourg again. He relents because Cosette is saddned when she does not see Marius. However, for the next three months Marius does not appear in the park so they stop going. Although she never speaks of her anguish, Cosette's sadness hurts Jean.

Aid From Below May Be Aid From Above

Summary

The only pleasures Jean and Cosette continue to share are their efforts to help the poor. It is at this time that they happen to visit the Jondrettes. Jean's wound keeps him indoors with a fever for a month. Cosette dresses it for him each day and urges him to see a doctor. He refuses, but finally tells her to call a "dog-doctor" to look at it. Cosette is so concerned about his wound that she spends all her time with him. Without noticing the change that is happening, she grows more content. Jean begins to recover by spring. One day she convinces him to walk in their beautiful garden. She is unaware that her gloom has lifted, but she is laughing and happy. When Jean fully recovers, he resumes his evening walks.

The End of Which Is Unlike the Beginning

Summary

One day Cosette is sitting in the garden on a seat which is hidden from the street. When she gets up, she notices a stone which was not there the moment before. Later, realizing that the stone must have been put there deliberately, she asks Toussaint if she is careful to lock the garden gates. Toussaint assures her that she locks everything well because they are two women alone. Despite these assurances, that night Cosette insists she double check all the doors and windows and inspect the house from top to bottom.

When Cosette awakens in the morning, she runs to the garden and looks under the stone. She finds a letter. There is no name on it, but she knows she must read it.

Although the letter has no name on it and no signature, she knows this message of love is from Marius and she kisses it after she reads it. She has fallen back into the romantic reverie of the time when she saw him daily in the park.

That evening Jean goes out and Cosette, without knowing why, fixes her hair and puts on a dress which is "a little immodest" because the neckline is slightly lower than those of her other dresses. She goes out to the garden. The stone is still there. She touches it and just then senses that someone is watching her. She turns and sees Marius. He confesses his love for her, she blushingly confides that she has loved him from afar. Finally, they tell each other their names.

Enchantments and Desolations

Summary

Marius is ecstatic, but he perceives a sadness in Cosette and asks what is troubling her. She tells him that her father informed her that morning that they might go to England. She suggests that Marius join them there, but he says he does not have enough money to do that. When she begins to sob, Marius tells her that he will die if she goes away. When he is about to leave, Marius tells her that he will not see her the following day. He scratches his address, 16, Rue de la Verrerie, into the plaster wall with his penknife.

Where Are They Going?

New Characters:

Gavroche: *Thénardier's son, one of the band of insurgents*

Bossuet, Feuilly, Combeferre, Joly, Bahorel: *revolutionists at the barricade*

Enjolras: *one of the commanders of the insurgents*

Summary

Increased police activity because of the political unrest in Paris and the fact that he has seen Thénardier several times in his neighborhood makes Jean nervous so he decides to leave the country and go to England. He plans to leave within a week. One morning he finds an address, 16, Rue de la Verrerie, scratched on his garden wall. He is sitting on the riverbank contemplating his fears when someone standing behind him drops a paper into his lap. A single word, "REMOVE," is written on the paper. Jean jumps up just in time to see a small man wearing a gray shirt running away. Jean goes home immediately.

Marius wanders aimlessly all day looking forward to his meeting with Cosette at 9 o'clock. As he walks to her home, he thinks he hears the sounds of fighting in the street. He is devastated when he finds her house and garden deserted. A voice through the trees which sounds like Eponine's advises him, "your friends are expecting you at the barricade, in the Rue de la Chanvrerie."

At the barricade, a torch protected from the wind on three sides sheds light only on the red flag of the insurgents.

It is evening, and there are few sounds of fighting while the government gathers an army of thousands. There are fifty men in

the barricade. Gavroche, the gamin (a gamin is a street urchin, a boy who roams the streets), is holding an infantry musket when Enjolras, one of the leaders, approaches him and asks him to go into the street and report what is happening. Gavroche points out a big man in their midst and accuses him of being a spy. When he is surrounded by four of the rebels, the spy confesses that he is Javert, a government official. They search him, finding a card which identifies him as a police inspector, and then tie him to a post in the basement of the wine shop. Others, including Courfeyrac, run in. Enjolras decrees that Javert "will be shot ten minutes before the barricade is taken."

Marius Enters the Shadow

Summary

Eponine's words are like a call of destiny to Marius. Like a man possessed, he hurries through silent streets, avoiding troops and sentinels until he comes close to the barricade where all is dark.

When he reaches the markets, he sees the red glare of the torch and moves toward it. Passing the sentry at the end of the street unnoticed, he rounds the last house and sees inside the barricade. He takes a last step into the barricade.

The Grandeurs of Despair

Summary

At ten o'clock Enjolras and Combeferre sit at the entrance of the barricade, listening for the sound of marching soldiers. Suddenly they hear Gavroche singing part of the song "Au clair de la lune" and know he is warning them. They watch him run down the empty street and leap into the barricade. Minutes later they hear the sound of many men marching toward them. A voice yells out asking them who they are and the insurgents yell back, "French Revolution." Fighting begins. There is an explosion in the barricade and several are wounded. There is a pause in the battle and Courfeyrac tells them not to waste their powder. They hear the troops reloading their weapons.

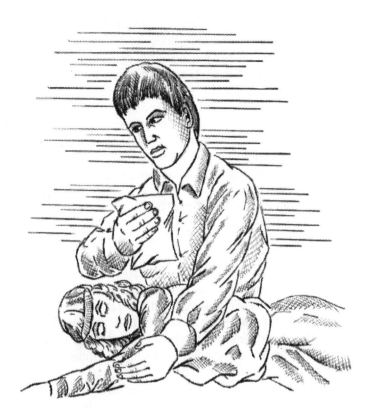

Alone on watch, Gavroche sounds the alarm when he hears men approaching the barricade. Municipal Guards overwhelm him. Bahorel, one of the rebels, kills the first one, but the second kills him. Another holds Courfeyrac on the ground with a bayonet but is shot in the head with a musket ball. A fourth guard is also struck. Marius has just entered the barricade.

Marius had been watching the battle from his hiding place. He rushes in with two pistols, saving Gavroche and Courfeyrac. Having used up his ammunition, he is now unarmed. A soldier aims at him and shoots, but Marius is saved by a young working-man who is shot when he jumps between Marius and the soldier. Marius sees a keg of powder on the ground but barely notices the person who saved him.

The insurgents rally. With their backs against the row of houses, they aim and fire at the approaching soldiers. Two explosions kill many on both sides. Marius yells, "Begone or I'll blow up the barricade" (240). During the confusion he has dragged the keg of powder to the end of the barricade near the torch. When the smoke clears, he is holding the torch, ready to light the keg. A soldier replies that he will also kill himself. When Marius yells that he will do it anyway, the soldiers flee, and the barricade is saved.

Marius asks where the chief is and is told by Enjolras that he is now the chief. The overwhelming joy Marius experienced for two short months has evaporated. He has lost Cosette and become the leader of the insurgents.

Marius goes to inspect the small barricade. As he is leaving, he hears a voice faintly calling him. He recognizes the voice of Eponine. She is dressed in men's clothing and lying in a pool of blood. It was she who was shot instead of Marius when he entered the barricade for the first time. She confesses that it was she who led him into the barricade even though she knew there would be no survivors. When she saw someone aiming at him, she took the bullet because she wanted to die before him. She also tells him that she has a letter for him. She was supposed to mail it, but she did not want him to receive it. She makes him promise that he will kiss her on the forehead when she is dead.

Keeping his promise, Marius kisses Eponine after she dies. He takes the letter. It is from Cosette. She tells him where she is and that she is leaving for England the following week.

Eponine has manipulated events. Hoping to separate Marius and Cosette, Eponine had warned Jean with the word "Remove," prompting him to decide to leave the country. Distraught, Cosette hastily wrote the note to Marius. She saw Eponine disguised as a boy, outside her garden gate and paid her five francs to deliver it. Eponine, hoping to come between Marius and Cosette, did not deliver the letter. Instead, she sent him a message to entice him into the barricade. She knew they would all die, but she was willing to go to her death and sacrifice Marius.

Marius now has two goals: to tell Cosette his fate and to save Gavroche who is Eponine's brother. He writes a letter to Cosette, telling her that although a lack of money kept them from marrying, they will be together soon because he is about to die. He puts the letter in his notebook. On the first page he writes his name and in-structions to take his body to his grandfather. He puts the book in his coat pocket, then gives the letter to Gavroche to deliver to Cosette.

The Rue de l'Homme Armé

Summary

When they leave their home on the Rue Plumet, Jean takes only the small box Cosette has christened "the inseparable"; Toussaint takes some linen and clothes, and Cosette brings her blotter and writing desk. Jean is in a moral dilemma because he cannot leave Toussaint behind, yet he cannot tell her why they must flee.

They arrive at their new quarters on the Rue de l'Homme Armé in the evening. The following day, Cosette remains in her room and returns without eating dinner claiming a headache. Several times Toussaint mentions that there is fighting in the streets, but Jean does not hear. Later, pacing about the room, he looks in the mirror and is stunned to read the letter Cosette had written to Marius earlier in the day. The words were on the blotter and the backward image is corrected when it reflects in the mirror. Chance has allowed Jean to read the letter before Marius. He is tortured by the loss his loved one will experience. When Toussaint returns, he asks her about the fighting in the street. Minutes later, he goes out.

Outside, he hears the attack on the barricade. Gavroche comes down the street. He sees but ignores Jean until Jean asks him what is the matter. He says he is hungry, and Jean gives him a five-franc note. Thanking him, Gavroche asks him to point out number seven. On a hunch, Jean asks Gavroche if he has brought him a letter. Gavroche protests that the letter is to be delivered to a woman, but Jean convinces him that he will take it to Cosette so he hands it over.

Jean takes the letter upstairs, lights a candle, and reads, "———— I die. When you read this, my soul will be near you." Inside, he is overjoyed. He is rid of Marius and he has not even had to do anything to achieve it. He soon becomes gloomy. About an hour later he goes out again. This time he is wearing the uniform of a National Guard and carrying a loaded musket. He walks in the direction of the barricade.

Saint Denis

Analysis

The love between Marius and Cosette continues to grow although from a distance. Having vacated his apartment, Marius lives in the Field of the Lark, a reference to a place on the bank of a brook as well as to the sphere of Cosette's influence. Cosette, it will be remembered, was called a lark in an earlier section of the novel.

A subplot with the theme of unrequited love develops between Marius and Eponine, who manipulates events on numerous occasions. Initially, she leads Marius to Cosette when he cannot find her. Later, she tries to keep them apart, disguising herself as a boy so Cosette will pay her to take a letter to Marius. She does not deliver it. Then, she drops a note in Jean's lap, frightening him into the decision to leave the country. Finally, she tells Marius that his friends expect him at the barricade. Knowing that he loves someone else and that her social status prevents a relationship with him in any case, she is willing to sacrifice both their lives.

St. Denis is a section of Paris where the barricade is located. An idyl is a poem which describes a simple or charming scene. Used in the title of this section, it refers to the garden scene at the house on the Rue Plumet where Marius declares his love for Cosette.

Action packed, this section uses a series of miscommunications and plot twists to bring the main characters together and set the stage for the final resolution of all of the plots and subplots.

Study Questions

1. Why does Jean rent the house in the Rue Plumet?

2. Why does Jean decide to leave the safety of the convent?

3. What events prompt Jean to decide to leave the country?

4. How does Eponine manipulate both Cosette and Marius?

5. To what degree are the men in the barricade outnumbered? What is the inevitable outcome of the battle?

6. Who is the spy in the barricade, and what is his fate?

7. How does Jean read the message Cosette sends to Marius even before Marius receives it?

8. How does Jean intercept the message Marius sends Cosette from the barricade and what does he do when he reads it?

9. What does Marius threaten to do if the soldiers do not retreat?

10. What does Marius write in his letter to Cosette?

Answers

1. He rents the house because it is located on a deserted street

and because it has a secret passage to an outside entrance a third of a mile away from the house. The passage will provide a safe exit if escape is necessary.

2.   Jean decides to leave the convent after Fauchelevent dies so that Cosette may have a more normal life.

3.   Two events convince Jean that he is in danger of being discovered. The first is that he finds an address scratched on his garden wall. He does not know that Marius wrote it there for Cosette. The other is that a paper with the word "REMOVE" written on it is dropped in his lap when he is sitting by the river. He does not know that it was written by Eponine, who was hoping to frighten him.

4.   Eponine manipulates them by not delivering a letter Cosette has paid her to take to Marius. Instead, she gives him a message that entices him to join his friends in the barricade.

5.   Since the government has an army of thousands and there are only fifty men in the barricade, the rebels all expect to die.

6.   Javert is the spy. When he is discovered, Enjolras has him tied to a post in the basement and says he will be executed just before the barricade is taken.

7.   An imprint of the letter is left on the blotter Cosette uses. Jean reads it by looking in a mirror which corrects the image.

8.   Gavroche is the gamin. Because of his small size, he is able to slip in and out of the barricade undetected so Marius gives him a letter to deliver to Cosette. He gives it, instead, to Jean. When Jean reads it, he joins the rebels in the barricade.

9.   Marius drags a keg of powder to the end of the barricade and threatens to blow it up if the soldiers do not retreat. He convinces them that he is serious when he acknowledges that he too will die if he ignites it.

10. He writes his name and states that he wants his body to be taken to his grandfather if he dies.

Suggested Essay Topics

1. Trace Cosette's evolution from the faithful daughter in the convent to a mature woman in love.

2. Discuss the theme of unrequited love regarding the relationship between Eponine and Marius. Why does Eponine pursue the relationship in spite of the fact that her love for him is doomed from the beginning?

3. In this portion of the novel, Jean is tormented by fear of losing Cosette and by fear of being discovered. What actions do these fears propel him to take?

4. Discuss the author's use of plot tricks to advance the action of the novel.

5. How does Marius emerge as the leader of the rebels?

Jean Valjean

War Between Four Walls

Summary

Enjolras tells the men they should leave the barricade if they do not wish to continue fighting, but they are surrounded by soldiers who will shoot anyone who tries to leave. Enjolras takes Combeferre into the basement room, and they return with four National Guard uniforms which can be worn to get out safely. Five men step forward. They debate which of them will take the uniforms but reach no conclusion. Unexpectedly, a fifth uniform is thrown on the pile by Jean Valjean who has easily passed through the streets wearing it. Marius recognizes him at once as M. Fauchelevent. He is invited to stay, but Enjolras warns him that they will all die.

The five men leave and the others build the barricade higher. They are fired upon and when the shells stop, Gavroche jumps back into the barricade.

Gavroche wants to replenish their supply of bullets, so he takes a basket from the wine shop and collects cartridge boxes from the 20 dead soldiers whose bodies are just outside the barricade. The fog and his small size protect him as he moves further into the street. Eventually, he is spotted and a bullet hits the body next to him. Another hits the pavement. The National Guard continue firing at him, always missing, and he mocks them, playing a hide-and-seek game with them. Those in the barricade watch breathlessly while he sings and dodges bullets. Eventually, he is struck.

Marius and Combeferre rush out to help him, but Gavroche is dead. Combeferre carries the basket while Marius brings the body back to the barricade. He is thinking that he is doing for Gavroche what Gavroche's father did for his father. The difference is that his father was alive when he was rescued by Thénardier. When Marius leans down to pick up the body, his head is grazed by a bullet. Courfeyrac takes off his scarf and ties it around the wound.

The barricade has been fortified again, and the wine shop made into the inner fortress. It is noon. Combeferre tells Marius to take watch outside. He says he will give the final orders from the wine shop. Turning to Javert, he tells him that he will not forget him. Placing a pistol on the table, he instructs the men that the last one out of the room should take Javert to the small barricade and execute him there so his body will not be found with theirs. Jean requests that he be rewarded by being the one to shoot Javert. Enjolras tells him to take the spy, and Jean picks up the pistol and cocks it.

Jean unties Javert's hands but leaves his feet bound. Leading him by a rope, he takes the prisoner to a small street at the end of the barricade near a pile of corpses of their fallen comrades. When

they are alone, Jean tells Javert who he is, and Javert responds by telling him to take his revenge. Jean cuts the ropes and tells him he is free to go. Although he does not expect to survive the battle, he gives Javert his address and the name he has been using. When Javert leaves, Jean fires the pistol in the air and returns to the barricade.

The barricade is assaulted again and again by the National Guards. Almost all of the rebels are killed or wounded, but after ten assaults, the barricade is still not taken. Bossuet, Feuilly, Courfeyrac, Joly, and Combeferre are all killed. Marius continues to fight in spite of multiple wounds. Only Enjolras is uninjured.

Enjolras and Marius are at opposite ends of the barricade. The leaders who were in the center are now all dead, and the barricade falls to the invaders. Marius is shot in the shoulder. His last thoughts are of Cosette and of his fear that he will be taken prisoner.

When Jean Valjean sees Marius fall, he picks him up and carries him, unnoticed, out of the barricade. He stops behind a house to rest and decide what to do. Noticing an iron grate in the pavement, Jean uses his enormous strength to open it and discovers an underground passage. As he lowers himself and the unconscious Marius into the darkness, he hears the sounds of the wine shop being overcome.

Mire, But Soul

Summary

Jean has descended into the dark and damp maze of the Paris sewer system. Marius hangs limply across his shoulders. After an hour of walking, Jean suddenly sees his shadow. He turns and sees a police star and eight or ten black forms following him.

On June 6, the government ordered the sewers to be searched. A lantern carried by one of the patrols on the left bank of the river casts a shadow on Jean. He stops and waits in the shadows close to the wall. The patrol, seeing nothing, passes by. As they leave, the sergeant fires in Jean's direction, striking the wall above his head.

Jean continues walking, but the journey becomes more and more difficult. The height of the arches supporting the sewer is only about five feet six inches forcing him to bend with each step so that Marius does not hit them. The slimy floor and damp walls also slow his progress. About 3 o'clock in the afternoon he reaches the Grand Sewer which is eight feet wide and seven feet high. He stops and gently lays Marius down. Tearing his shirt, he bandages Marius' wounds although he looks at him with hatred in his eyes. In Marius' pockets he finds a crust of bread, which he eats, and a pocket-book. Opening it, he reads Marius' instructions to take his corpse to his

grandfather. He replaces the pocket-book. Lifting Marius onto his shoulders, he descends again into the sewers.

Jean finds himself in a basin of water caused by the rain of the previous day. The soil beneath the streets near the Seine River is quicksand; heavy rain had caused the sinking of the pavement. Jean continues through water and slime up to his armpits. Though only his head is out of the water, he is still carrying Marius. As he reaches a depth which forces him to tilt his head back to breathe, he feels something solid beneath his feet and he begins reascending. He trips coming out of the water and falls on his knees. Remaining on his knees, he prays. When he finally rises, his soul is "filled with a strange light."

Jean presses on desperately. He finally reaches the outlet and sees daylight, but he cannot get out. The opening is covered by a grate fastened by a double lock. Jean frantically tries to break through the bars, but they do not bend. Exhausted and dejected, he sinks to the ground. He thinks about Cosette.

In the midst of his despair, he hears a voice say, "Go halves." He recognizes Thénardier, but Thénardier does not recognize him. Thénardier assumes Jean is a common criminal who has killed for money. He proposes a trade: he will unlock the grate if Jean will give him half of what is in his pockets. He also offers a rope and tells Jean that he will find a stone outside so he can tie up the body and throw it into the river.

Jean usually carries a lot of money, but he has forgotten his pocket-book and has only a small amount of money. Thénardier comments that he has not killed for much and takes the entire sum. He unlocks the grate, and Jean carries Marius out. Thénardier closes the grate, relocks it, and disappears into the darkness.

Jean lays Marius on the beach and bathes his face with water. He appears dead but is breathing slightly. Jean dips his hand into the river again. He senses that someone is watching. He turns and finds Javert behind him. Javert does not recognize him either, but Jean reveals his identity and tells him that he is his prisoner. He asks only that Javert permit him to carry Marius home. Javert also thinks Marius is dead, but Jean says he is not. Jean takes out Marius' pocket-book and finds the address Marius has written in it. Javert keeps the pocket-book and the three of them get into a carriage.

When the carriage arrives at M. Gillenormand's house, every-one is asleep. They tell the porter they have brought Marius home and carry him upstairs. A doctor is called. Jean and Javert return to the carriage and Jean makes one more request. He wants to return to his home on the Rue de l'Homme Armé briefly. Then, he prom-ises, Javert can do what he wants with him.

The carriage stops at the end of his deserted street because it is too narrow for carriages. At the door, Javert tells Jean to go in. When he gets to the top of the stairs, he looks out the window and is amazed to find that Javert is gone.

A doctor examines Marius to determine the extent of his wounds. A bullet deflected by his pocket-book has torn up his ribs, his shoulder is dislocated, and he has superficial head and face wounds; but he has no internal injuries, and his face is not disfig-ured. When his grandfather sees him, he bends over him, over-whelmed by the sight of his wounds, and mournfully cries out. He thinks his grandson is dead, but Marius opens his eyes and looks at him. The grandfather expresses his joy, calls Marius his son, and faints from the excitement.

Javert Off The Track

Summary

When Javert leaves Jean's house, he walks to the Seine River, reflecting on what has transpired. He is in a state of mental tor-ment because all of his values and beliefs have crumbled. He is astounded that Jean spared his life and frightened because he in return has spared Jean. He remembers Jean's acts of kindness and reluctantly realizes that he has come to admire the convict. He sees only two ways out of his moral dilemma. One is to recapture Jean and return him to the galleys. He leans over the railing and watches the swirling waters beneath him and chooses the other alterna-tive. He plunges into the Seine.

The Grandson And The Grandfather

Summary

In his delirium, Marius calls out for Cosette. He is visited daily by a well dressed gentleman with white hair. Finally, after four months, the doctor declares that he is out of danger, but he continues to recuperate for another two months. As his health improves, his problems with his grandfather resurface. He mentally prepares himself for a battle with the old man because he has vowed to himself that he will either have Cosette or die. If his grandfather denies him, he plans to tear off his bandages, reopen his wounds, and refuse to eat.

Marius tells his grandfather that he wishes to marry. Gillenormand tells him that he has foreseen this event and that Marius should marry. In an emotional exchange, Marius calls him "father," and the old man realizes that Marius does love him. He tells Marius that Cosette will be brought to him the next day.

Cosette and M. Fauchelevent, who carries a package wrapped in paper under his arm, visit Marius. The grandfather explains to Mademoiselle Gillenormand that Fauchelevent is a scholar and is carrying books. On behalf of his grandson, he asks Fauchelevent for his daughter's hand. When permission is granted, he tells the couple they have permission to "adore" one another.

The grandfather praises Cosette and tells the couple how right they are for each other. He says it is a pity that most of his money is in an annuity which they will not get until 20 years after his death. Fauchelevent interrupts and tells them that Euphrasie Fauchelevent has almost 600,000 francs. He explains that Euphrasie is Cosette's real name. He unwraps the package he is carrying and counts out 584,000 thousand francs.

Long ago, when Jean left M——sur M——, he withdrew his money from Laffitte's Bank and buried 630,000 francs and the bishop's silver candlesticks in a chest in the forest of Montfermeil in a place called Blaru glade. Whenever he needed money, he would visit the glade. He had recently retrieved the chest. He took 500 francs for himself and gave 584,000 for Cosette. The balance had been spent on living expenses for the past ten years from 1823 to 1833. It had cost them only 5000 francs for the five years they lived at the convent. Jean puts the silver candlesticks on his mantel.

Jean learns that he is free of Javert, whose death by drowning has been reported in the newspaper.

Happiness prevails as they prepare for the wedding. Jean's experience as mayor has given him the knowledge to handle the matter of Cosette's background. Since admitting the truth might jeopardize the marriage, he invents a family for her and has a notary draw up papers, declaring that she is Mademoiselle Euphrasie Fauchelevent, the orphan daughter of his brother. Jean also arranges it so that he will remain her guardian and M. Gillenormand will be her overseeing guardian. He explains her fortune by saying that it was left to her by a relative who wishes to remain anonymous. It is to be given to her when she marries or becomes of legal age.

Had Cosette been told this story of her heritage at any other time, she might have been devastated to learn that the man she thinks of as her father is merely a relative. However, this unexpected news is overshadowed by her bliss, and she continues to call Jean "father."

The young couple will live with the grandfather who vacates his own room because it is the best in the house and fills it with fine furniture for them. His library becomes the attorney's office.

Cosette and Fauchelevent visit Marius every day. It is unusual for the bride-to-be to visit the groom, but the habit was begun when Marius was still recuperating from his injuries. Marius and Fauchelevent do not speak to one another, but it is necessary for him to accompany her as her chaperone.

Marius regards him as cold although he accepts his presence as a part of loving Cosette. His memory of the past is vague. He questions whether it is possible that he really saw Fauchelevent at the barricade, but his relationship with the man prevents him from discussing it. Once, he attempted discussion by asking Fauchelevent if he knew the location of the Rue de la Chanvrerie. When Fauchelevent replies that he never heard of it, Marius is convinced that the person he recalled merely looked like Fauchelevent.

While preparations are being made for the wedding, Marius does some investigating. He owes debts to Thénardier because of his father and to the unknown person who saved him. Thénardier's wife had died in prison, but he and his daughter Azelma disappeared without a trace. Investigators manage to locate the carriage that delivered Marius to his grandfather. The driver reveals that he picked up Marius, the man who was carrying him, and an officer near the Grand Sewer at nine o'clock on the evening of June 6. After leaving Marius at home, the driver then took the other two to a street near the Archives where they departed. He knew nothing else.

Marius remembers nothing from the time he fell in the barricade until he regained consciousness at his grandfather's. He still has the clothing he was wearing that night. He examines it and finds that the coat is torn and a piece of it is missing.

One evening Marius tells Cosette and Fauchelevent about the frustration of his search. Angered by Fauchelevent's indifference, he explains how much he owes the stranger who bravely carried him four miles through the slimy sewers. To Marius he was like the archangel and he claims he would gladly give Cosette's entire fortune to find him.

The White Night

Summary

It is a blessed night because it is the wedding night for Marius and Cosette. The night before, in the presence of his grandfather, Jean had given Marius the 584,000 thousand francs. A few days before, Jean had injured the thumb on his right hand. The injury is not serious so he bandages it and wears a sling so he is unable to sign any documents at the marriage ceremony. The necessary papers are signed by M. Gillenormand as Cosette's overseeing guardian.

Cosette is strikingly beautiful on the day of her wedding. She and her handsome bridegroom become Monsieur the Baron and Madame the Baroness and are admired by all. After exchanging vows and rings and signing both municipal and church documents, they are taken by carriage to their home, with Jean and the grandfather riding in the back, to their wedding banquet. She is tender toward Jean, speaking to him in the voice she used as a girl, and he tells her he is pleased. A chair is reserved on one side of the bride

for the grandfather and on the other side for Jean, but when they are seated, Jean is absent. Basque, the servant, informs them that Jean left because his hand was causing him great pain. He asked to be excused and left a message that he would visit the following day.

After an uncomfortable moment, the grandfather declares that Jean was right to leave if he was suffering and invites Marius to take his place by Cosette's side. Though Cosette is at first sad that Jean is not there, it pleases her to be next to Marius and within minutes gaiety is restored.

Jean returns to an empty home. Even Toussaint is gone. He wanders through vacant rooms, looks at the naked beds and opens closets. Cosette's room is empty, stripped of her personal things. He goes into his own room and takes off the sling. His hand is not really injured. On his bed is "the inseparable," the small trunk which made Cosette jealous. He had put it there on June 4 when he arrived in the Rue de l'Homme Armé.

He takes out the key, opens it, and removes the black clothing Cosette wore when she left Montfermeil. He remembers the winter ten years past when he had taken her, ragged and thin, and dressed her in these mourning clothes. He recalls their journey through the forest and pictures her as a child when she had no one to care for her but him. Fingering the clothing, his heart breaking, he sobs.

Marius and Cosette are wealthy and happy, but Jean does not know what he should do. Once again, his past causes him anguish as he lies in bed all night contemplating what his role should be in their lives. He wonders if he should be the "ominous mute of destiny" in the lives of the happy couple. Motionless and silent for twelve hours, he appears to be dead until he suddenly kisses Cosette's clothes.

The Last Drop In The Chalice

Summary

The newlyweds sleep late the morning after the wedding. Basque, hearing a tap, opens the door for M. Fauchelevent, who asks if his master is awake. Basque says he will tell Monsieur the Baron that M. Fauchelevent is calling, but Jean tells him to say only that someone wishes to speak with him in private.

When Marius sees who it is, he says, "It is you, father!" Jean is pleased that the barrier between them is dissolving and that Marius thinks of him as a father. Marius says he is happy to see that the hand is better and tells Jean that he must come and live with them.

Jean confesses that he is a convict and that there was never anything wrong with his hand. He explains that he invented the injury so that he would not have to commit forgery by signing anything at the wedding. Marius is shocked. He is further astounded when Jean reveals that his name is not Fauchelevent but Jean Valjean and that he is not even related to Cosette. Marius does not want to believe him but, studying Jean's calm demeanor, accepts his word.

Jean further explains how Cosette came into his life and then says that as of this day, he is leaving her life. She is now Madame Pontmercy and no longer needs him. He is driven by honor and conscience to confess his past to Marius. He is, he says, an honest man, "a galley slave who obeys his conscience" (305). He once stole a loaf of bread to survive, but he can no longer go on stealing a name in order to live.

Marius takes his hand and suggests that he can get his grandfather to procure a pardon, but Jean reminds him that the authorities think he is dead. He asks that Marius not tell Cosette his secret, then covers his face with his hands and weeps. He asks Marius to keep his secret, and they decide that it would be best if Jean did not see Cosette that day. As he is leaving, Jean asks permission to visit Cosette from time to time, and Marius tells him to come every evening.

Marius is overwhelmed by Jean's disgraceful past. His confession explains the negative feelings Marius instinctively felt in the past. Reflecting on Jean's presence in the barricade, he recalls that it was Jean who dragged Javert out of the barricade to be executed and assumes that Jean's reason for being there was to rid himself of his enemy. Marius wonders how it is that fate has tied this man to Cosette.

The Twilight Wane

Summary

The following evening, Jean visits Cosette. He enters through the coach door and tells Basque that he wishes to remain in the basement room. Having neither eaten nor slept for several days, he is exhausted and sinks into one of two chairs next to the fireplace. Cosette enters and he marvels at her beauty. She asks why he wishes to visit with her in the basement, and he tells her it is just his whim. He refers to her as "madame" and tells her not to call him father any more, but, rather, to address him as Monsieur Jean.

She says she will ask her husband's permission to call him Monsieur Jean although she does not understand why it must be so. She tells him that he should not cause her grief and asks if he likes her being so happy. Almost to himself, he replies that her happiness has been the whole reason for his life. He says, "Cosette, you are happy; my time is full." She is pleased that he has called her by her name and embraces him. He passionately returns the embrace as if she is his once again but then pushes her away. He tells her to tell her husband he will not use her name again and returns to being formal. She is confused by his behavior.

Jean visits the next day at the same time. Cosette lets him talk and doesn't ask any questions. She does not call him father or Monsieur Jean. He visits every day at the same hour, and Marius arranges his schedule so he is not home then.

Several weeks pass and Cosette becomes accustomed to married life. Her sole pleasure is being with Marius. She becomes detached from Jean but she still loves him very much. Jean continues to live in the same place because he doesn't want to be farther away from her. Gradually his visits get longer. One day Cosette calls him father and his face lights up. Turning away so she cannot see him wipe away a tear, he reminds her to call him Jean.

In the spring and summer of 1833, the residents of the Rue de l'Homme Armé observe an old man dressed in black, walking to the corner of the Rue des Filles du Calvaire. His happiness is apparent as he approaches; but when he arrives at the corner, he is gloomy and has tears in his eyes. He stays for a few minutes and returns. Though he comes out of his house at the same time each day, over time he shortens the distance he travels, no longer walking all the way to the corner. His eyes are dull and he no longer has tears.

Supreme Shadow, Supreme Dawn

New Characters:

The Portress: *servant in Jean's building*

The Physician: *attends Jean*

Summary

Marius asks Jean no questions but gradually banishes him from his home and tries to make Cosette forget him. He meets an old man who was a clerk at Laffitte's and learns some information which he does not understand but which compels him to avoid spending any of the 584,000 francs. In the meantime, he quietly searches for the person he thinks is the rightful owner.

One day Jean goes out but returns after walking only a few steps. The next day he stays inside, and the following day he stays in bed. After a week he is still in bed. When the portress sees a doctor at the end of the street, she sends him up to see Jean. The physician reports that Jean is very sick, that he seems to have lost a dear friend, and that he might die.

One day Jean awakens to find himself weaker. With a supreme effort, he gets up and dresses. He takes out Cosette's clothes and spreads them on the bed. He lights the bishop's candlesticks. Seeing his reflection in the mirror, he notes that he now looks 80 years old. Just a year ago, before Cosette's wedding, he looked only 50.

By nightfall, the effort of moving a chair and table near the fireplace causes him to faint. When he regains consciousness, he writes a letter to Cosette explaining the story of the jet factory so she will know the money honestly belongs to her. Exhausted by the effort, he tells himself that he does not mind dying, but he does mind dying without seeing Cosette once more and laments that he will never see her again. There is a knock at the door.

That same evening Basque hands Marius a letter signed by Baron Thénard who claims to know secrets about someone close to Marius. Marius tells Basque to show him in. The Baron tells Marius about Jean Valjean, and Marius replies that he already knows everything about him.

The Baron then offers information about Cosette's fortune for 20,000 francs. When Marius says that he knows this too, the Baron reduces his price to 10,000 francs. Marius refuses but the Baron persists, saying that he will talk for 20 francs. Marius identifies the Baron as Thénardier and says he knows that Jean is an assassin because he killed Javert and a thief who stole a fortune from M. Madeleine. Thénardier reveals that he is wrong, that Jean is M. Madeleine, and that Javert committed suicide. When Marius tells him to prove it, Thénardier produces two old newspapers which

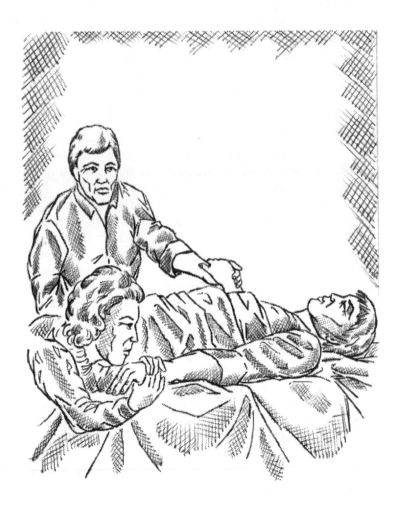

verify his story. Marius cries out in joy. Jean is a hero and a saint.

Thénardier insists that Jean is still a robber and a murderer and tells Marius about his encounter with Jean in the Grand Sewer when Jean was carrying the corpse of a man he robbed and killed. Thénardier produces a piece of cloth cut from the coat of the corpse. At this news, Marius pales. He grabs the piece of fabric and matches it to the coat he was wearing the night he was delivered to his grandfather. It fits exactly. He angrily tells Thénardier that he knows he is Jondrette. The only thing protecting him is the fact that he saved Marius' father at Waterloo. Marius tells him he will see that he leaves for America the next day with his daughter. Then he will give him another 20,000 francs.

Two days later Thénardier, using a new name, and his daughter do leave for America with 20,000 francs. Morally irredeemable, Thénardier uses the money to become a slave trader.

The moment Thénardier leaves, Marius, greatly excited, orders a coach and calls Cosette. The two race off to Jean's house. On the way, he explains that it was Jean who saved him and spared Javert in the barricade. Since Cosette never received the letter he sent her from the barricade, he assumes, correctly, that Gavroche must have given it to Jean.

When they arrive, Cosette kisses Jean, and he says he thought he would never see her again. He asks Marius to forgive him, but Marius protests. He owes his life to Jean whom he calls his angel. He asks Jean why he did not tell the whole truth. Jean replies that Marius was right to want him to go away, so he didn't want to embarrass him. Marius protests that Jean must now come to live with them, but Jean says that he will die soon, that God also thinks he should go away.

The physician comes in. Feeling Jean's pulse, he comments that Jean needed to see Cosette and whispers to Marius that it is too late. Struggling to rise, Jean takes the crucifix from the wall and puts it on the table. He kisses Cosette's sleeve and explains to Marius that Cosette's money really belongs to her and tells briefly how it was earned. The physician asks Jean if he wants a priest, and he says that he already has one. "It is probable that the Bishop was indeed a witness of this death-agony."

Weakening, he speaks to them in a whisper, saying that he

wants Cosette to have fine things. He gives her the silver candle-sticks and asks to be buried under a stone with no name on it. He hopes that Cosette will visit the spot occasionally and that Marius will too. Although he has not always loved Marius, he loves him now because he makes Cosette so happy. He tells Cosette about her mother, Fantine, and how unhappy her life was. He advises them always to love one another because that is all there is in this world. He sees a light and invites them to move closer. Tearfully, they each hold one hand, covering it with kisses, and he dies.

There is a stone in the cemetery near the Potters' field. Like all other stones, it is ravaged by time and the elements. No path leads to it, and no one walks near it because of the high grass. Large enough to cover a man, the stone bears no name.

Jean Valjean

Analysis

With its escape scenes through the Paris sewers, this is the most famous portion of the novel. Jean's monumental efforts to save Marius catapult him into true heroism. Though he despises this man who threatens to take his beloved Cosette away from him, he is willing to sacrifice himself for her happiness. His journey through the filthy sewer, fraught with danger, is a symbol for the trials he has had to surmount throughout his entire life. When Marius is returned to his family, he is referred to as the prodigal son and, as in the Bible, he is forgiven and welcomed back.

The author uses this section of the novel to tie all of the plots and subplots together and offer some resolutions. Marius and Cosette, basking in the glow of their love for one another, become the hope for the future. The rebels have fallen, indicating not that their cause is unworthy, but that social and political change require more than a single battle. Javert, the symbol of law and order, comes to admire Jean. Caught between his sense of duty and his sense of justice, he takes his own life. Thénardier's entry into the slave trade proves that he is inherently evil and that the mere acquisition of money does not improve the values of the corrupt.

Having been relentlessly pursued all of his life, Jean finally reaches a state of peace and love. He has won the battle and achieved his goal of moving closer to God. In spite of the fact that circumstances have forced him to lie about his identity, he is truly an honest man. His story is epic-like in that he has been on a life-long quest to reach a state of grace.

Study Questions

1. How does the relationship between Gavroche and Marius compare to the relationship between Pontmercy and Thénardier?

2. How does M. Gillerormand react to Cosette and Marius' marriage?

3. What is the final outcome of the battle at the barricade?

4. What obstacles does Jean encounter as he carries Marius through the sewers of Paris?

5. Why does Javert commit suicide?

6. Why does Jean pretend to have an injury when Cosette gets married?

7. Why is Jean despondent after Cosette's wedding?

8. What evidence does Thénardier produce to prove that he is telling Marius the truth?

9. How does Marius resolve his obligation to Thénardier?

10. What final requests does Jean make before he dies?

Answers

1. Both Marius and Thénardier risk their lives to rescue a fallen comrade. When Gavroche is shot, Marius carries his body back to the barricade just as Thénardier carried Pontmercy to safety when he was injured in battle. The difference is that Pontmercy was still alive when Thénardier rescued him.

2. He invites Marius and Cosette to live with him. He gives up his own room for them and fills it with fine furniture.

3. The soldiers break through the barricade and kill most of the rebels. Jean sees Marius fall and carries him to safety.

4. The dampness of the sewer makes it slippery, and the darkness makes it difficult for Jean to find his way. The low ceilings make it necessary for him to bend with each step, and he is physically exhausted from carrying the unconscious Marius across his shoulders. At one point, he must wade through water and slime up to his neck. When he finally reaches an opening, he finds that it is covered by a locked grate.

5. Javert commits suicide because all of his values have collapsed. He has reluctantly come to admire the man he has spent his life pursuing.

6. Jean pretends to injure the thumb on his right hand so that he will not have to commit forgery by signing any documents. Since the authorities think he is dead, he is afraid that the marriage will not be legal if he signs them.

7. Jean is heartbroken because he feels that he has lost Cosette, the only person he has ever loved.

8. Thénardier produces a newspaper which reports the suicide of Javert and a piece of cloth that was torn from Marius' coat.

9. Marius satisfies his obligation to Thénardier by giving him 20,000 francs and sending him to America with his daughter.

10. He tells Marius and Cosette to love one another and asks to be buried under a stone with no name on it.

Suggested Essay Topics

1. Discuss the importance of Jean's journey through the sewers. What is its symbolism and what is his motivation?

2. Discuss the parent-child relationship that exists between Cosette and Jean and Marius and Gillenormand. What steps are taken by Jean and Gillenormand to ensure the happy marriage of Cosette and Marius?

3. Why is Jean so despondent toward the end of the novel?

4. Thénardier is a character the author uses to represent the evils of society. At the end of the novel, he attempts to blackmail Marius. How does the author resolve the situation? Explain whether or not this is a fitting end.

Sample Analytical Paper Topics

The following paper topics are based on the entire novel. Following each topic is a thesis and sample outline. Use these as a starting point for your paper.

Topic #1

Discuss the ways in which Jean Valjean finds redemption in the course of the novel. How is Jean Valjean an honorable man?

Outline

I. Thesis Statement: *Through his actions, Jean Valjean seeks to redeem himself for past crimes and becomes an honorable man.*

II. Jean's decision to seek redemption

   A. Past crimes

   B. The influence of the bishop.

III. The path to redemption

   A. Jean resurrects M—— sur M—— and becomes a respected citizen

   B. The rescue of Fauchelevent

   C. The Champmathieu affair

    D. Jean loves and cares for Cosette

    E. Acts of charity

    F. Jean spares Javert

    G. Jean rescues Marius

Topic #2

How does Hugo express human misery in *Les Misérables*?

Outline

  I. Thesis Statement: *Both the unfortunate and the infamous experience misery in the novel.*

 II. The misery of man.

    A. Jean Valjean.

    B. Thénardier.

III. The misery of women.

    A. Fantine.

    B. Thénardier's wife.

IV. The misery of children.

    A. Eponine and Azelma.

    B. Cosette.

Topic #3

Discuss the bravery and courage of the characters in the novel.

Outline

  I. Thesis Statement: *Hugo's characters exhibit courage in battle and in their daily lives.*

 II. Bravery in the barricade.

    A. The rebels fight although they know they cannot win the battle.

    B. Marius saves the barricade and risks his life to help Gavroche.

      C. Gavroche dies collecting cartridge boxes

      D. Eponine intercepts a bullet meant for Marius.

      E. Jean spares Javert.

III. The courage of Jean Valjean.

      A. The rescue of Fauchelevent.

      B. Jean's testimony saves Champmathieu

      C. The risk of caring for Cosette

      D. Saving Marius

Topic #4

How does Hugo portray women in the novel? How is this a reflection of the historical context of the novel?

Outline

I. Thesis Statement: *Women are dominated by the men in their lives and treated as second-class citizens in the novel. None of the women in the novel achieve true independence.*

      A. Fantine

         1. Her social condition

         2. The pain of leaving her child

      B. Cosette

         1. The faithful daughter

         2. Her relationship with Marius

         3. Finds happiness, but even she continues to be dominated by the men in her life

      C. The downtrodden Thénardiers

         1. The wife is ruled by her husband

         2. Eponine reaches for independence

         3. Azelma remains with her father

      D. Gillenormand's daughters

1. The eldest remains unmarried and under her father's influence

2. The younger marries the man she loves in spite of her father's opposition

Topic #5

Discuss how Hugo employs the sewers as a symbolic device and metaphor.

Outline

I. Thesis Statement: *The escape through the sewers symbolizes Jean's journey toward redemption.*

II. Overcoming obstacles on the journey

   A. Low ceilings force him to bend over and grope his way through the passage

   B. Jean tries to find his way through the darkness

   C. Slippery footing

   D. Jean carries Marius and the weight of his sins on his back

   E. The danger of drowning

III. Encountering Thénardier

SECTION EIGHT

Bibliography

Cairns, Trevor. *The Old Regime and the Revolution*. Minneapolis: Lerner Publications Co., 1980.

Chalfont, Lord, ed. *Waterloo: Battle of Three Armies*. New York: Alfred A. Knopf, 1980.

Davidson, Marshall B. *The Horizon Concise History of France*. New York: American Heritage Publishing Co., Inc., 1971.

Hugo, Victor. *Les Misérables*. Abridged with an introduction by James K. Robinson. New York: Fawcett Premier, 1961.

Kelly, Linda. *The Young Romantics*. New York: Random House, 1976.

Lewis, Gynne. *Life in Revolutionary France*. New York: G. P. Putnam's Sons, 1972.

Thibaudet, Albert. *French Literature from 1795 to Our Era*. New York: Funk & Wagnalls, 1967.

Introducing...

MAXnotes

REA's Literature Study Guides

MAXnotes™ offer a fresh look at masterpieces of literature, presented in a and interesting fashion. **MAXnotes**™ offer the essentials of what you should about the work, including outlines, explanations and discussions of the character lists, analyses, and historical context. **MAXnotes**™ are designed to you think independently about literary works by raising various issues and tho provoking ideas and questions. Written by literary experts who currently teach subject, **MAXnotes**™ enhance your understanding and enjoyment of the wor

---

Available **MAXnotes**™ include the following:

Gone With The Wind
by Margaret Mitchell

The Grapes of Wrath
by John Steinbeck

Great Expectations
by Charles Dickens

The Great Gatsby
by F. Scott Fitzgerald

Hamlet
by William Shakespeare

Huckleberry Finn
by Mark Twain

**I Know Why the
Caged Bird Sings**
by Maya Angelou

Julius Caesar
by William Shakespeare

Les Misèrables
by Victor Hugo

Macbeth
by William Shakespeare

The Odyssey
by Homer

A Raisin in the Sun
by Lorraine Hansberry

The Scarlet Letter
by Nathaniel Hawthorn

A Tale of Two Cities
by Charles Dickens

To Kill a Mockingbird
by Harper Lee

RESEARCH & EDUCATION ASSOCIATION
61 Ethel Road W. • Piscataway, New Jersey 08854
Phone: (908) 819-8880

Please send me more information about MAXnotes™.

Name _____

Address _____

City _____ State _____ Zip _____

The High School Tutor

The **HIGH SCHOOL TUTORS** series is based on the same principle as the comprehensive **PROBLEM SOLVERS,** but is specifically designed to meet the need high school students. REA has recently revised all the books in this series to include expan review sections, new material, and newly-designed covers. This makes the books even r effective in helping students to cope with these difficult high school subjects.